"This is not a book—it is a life raft, a survival kit, and a refuge. Mark C. Purcell and Jason R. Murphy have offered us the most precious gifts possible: tools for finding inner freedom and meditation techniques that will surely lead to a greater sense of happiness and well-being. *Mindfulness for Teen Anger* is the book I needed as a confused youth sitting in juvenile hall trying to figure out how to save my own life with meditation."

> —**Noah Levine**, author of *Dharma Punx, Against the Stream, Heart of the Revolution,* and *Refuge Recovery*

"At last, a nonjudgmental and systematic approach for dealing with anger! This comprehensive and wise workbook offers an array of practical tools and meditations to help understand, work with, and transform our anger. It's geared to teens but truly useful for any age."

> —**Diana Winston**, director of mindfulness education, UCLA Mindful Awareness Research Center, and author of *Fully Present: The Science, Art, and Practice of Mindfulness*

"This book fills an important gap in the treatment landscape for teens. Many teens have difficulties managing anger and its attendant urges and behaviors, but not everyone has access to the relief that mindfulness and other DBT skills can bring. The idea of an 'instant help' book for teens is a perfect format for today's fast-paced world, and Murphy and Purcell have helpfully broken up complex concepts into easily digestible chunks for any teenager who is even slightly open to decreasing their anger and aggression. Highly recommended."

> —**Esme A.L. Shaller, PhD**, director of the dialectical behavior therapy program at University of California, San Francisco, and assistant clinical professor at University of California, San Francisco and Berkeley

"*Mindfulness for Teen Anger* is an important book to help one live better with anger. Through down-to-earth stories and practical exercises and skills, one can learn to transform anger into deeper understanding and peace. This book will be highly recommended to any teen living with anger and hostility who wants to get at its root cause to live a freer and happier life."

—**Bob Stahl, PhD**, coauthor of *A Mindfulness-Based Stress Reduction Workbook, Living with Your Heart Wide Open, Calming the Rush of Panic,* and *A Mindfulness-Based Stress Reduction Workbook for Anxiety*

"This is a great book. Anger is a normal part of growing up, but everyone can master skills to cope with such a stressful emotion. This book helps readers understand anger and how to master it. The simple exercises coach teens to develop healthy emotional coping skills. This book is a fabulous resource."

—**Kellen Glinder, MD**, pediatrician and department chair at the Palo Alto office of the Palo Alto Medical Foundation

"*Mindfulness for Teen Anger* is one of the most comprehensive approaches to adolescent anger I have found. It not only provides practical tools to help teens understand and manage their anger, but goes deeper to help them develop emotional resilience. Using real-life examples and an engaging style, this book teaches teens how to improve their emotional control with strategies ranging from 'trusting your wise mind' and thinking 'cool thoughts,' to practicing guided meditations and assertive communication. This book is so much more than just an anger management workbook; it is an instruction manual for social and emotional health."

—**Holly Pedersen, PhD, MFT**, director of community education and the bullying prevention program at Jewish Children and Family Services in Palo Alto, CA

"*Mindfulness for Teen Anger* is the kind of book I would recommend because it is truly directed at a teen. It talks *to* you, not at you like so many other teen workbooks. In addition, it gives information and ideas, allowing the reader to draw their own conclusions about their actions, reactions, thoughts, and feelings. It is a versatile book—one that could be read and used by teens alone, one that could help parents, one a therapist could use with a teen, one a teacher could use with a class, and the list goes on."

> —**Susan M. Howe, LMFT**, licensed marriage and family therapist and director of transitional age youth services at Edgewood Center for Children and Families

"After reviewing this book I was very excited about the potential it has to help children cope with and regulate their emotions. It provides a very good source workbook for any teen trying to understand and work through anger issues. The key to controlling anger is in our thinking. The approach in this book helps teens [cultivate] mindfulness, which allows them to pay attention to the present and observe and understand their thoughts and feelings. This awakens them to their experiences in a very pragmatic way. I highly recommend this book to anyone interested in helping a teenager cope with anger and aggression. It is practical and understandable, and will provide direct assistance to teens in establishing the thought control necessary to change their behavior.

> —**Joseph J. Cozzo MA, MS, LMHC**, president and CEO at Buffalo Hearing & Speech Center

"An easy-to-read manual for adolescents dealing with anger problems. There is a great need for a self-help book like this for dealing with anger. A practical and accessible guide."

> —**Omid J. Naim, MD**, adult, child, and adolescent psychiatrist at Hope Integrative Psychiatry

"This is an immensely useful resource for both psychotherapists and clients. [Purcell and Murphy's] book provides an excellent explication of cutting-edge knowledge of the mindfulness approach and its value for effective treatment of adolescent issues. We in the mental health profession will be grateful beneficiaries in years to come."

> —**Benjamin R. Tong, PhD**, professor of clinical psychology at the California Institute of Integral Studies

mindfulness for
teen anger

---

a workbook to
overcome anger &
aggression using
MBSR & DBT skills

MARK C. PURCELL, MEd, PsyD
JASON R. MURPHY, MA

Instant Help Books
An Imprint of New Harbinger Publications, Inc.

Publisher's Note

This publication is designed to provide accurate and authoritative information in regard to the subject matter covered. It is sold with the understanding that the publisher is not engaged in rendering psychological, financial, legal, or other professional services. If expert assistance or counseling is needed, the services of a competent professional should be sought.

Distributed in Canada by Raincoast Books

Cover design by Amy Shoup
Acquired by Tesilya Hanauer
Edited by Karen Schader

Library of Congress Cataloging-in-Publication Data on file

Printed in the United States of America

18   17   16

15   14   13   12   11   10   9   8   7

This book is dedicated to all those who have helped me along this path; to those who pointed the way when I was lost. King Gaskins, Robyn Claire Wesley, Badri Dass, Tom B, Walter Guzman, Noah Levine, Bob Stahl and Mary Grace Orr, to name a few. Without your love, support and guidance, who knows where I would be.

I also dedicate this book to the many young warriors of the Y.E.S school, and all those who have let me witness their courageous hearts—I see you.

—Jason Murphy

I would like to express gratitude to my guides along the way: Ben Tong, Paul Wanner, Joe Herlicy, Kathy Mulherin, Bob Selman, Edward "Doc" Eismann, Bob Stahl, Jim Casion, and Joe Cozzo, along with Susan Howe and the rest of my DBT gang. I am grateful for the unconditional support of my parents, my wife Veronica, and my children. I owe so much of who I am to what you have taught me through your compassion and inspiring deeds. Most importantly, I extend my deep appreciation to the young people who I have been privileged to work with; more than anyone, you have shown me what truly works.

—Mark Purcell

contents

introduction

How is reading some workbook going to help you? That's exactly what we thought when we were your age. One thing is certain: our own lives are different today because of the ways we learned to look at, deal with, and let go of anger. In this book you'll find helpful tools to overcome anger and aggressive behavior that just might be getting in the way of your happiness.

We have developed these tools from three approaches:

1. The work of Ronald and Patricia Potter-Efron (2006)—activity 1

2. Dialectical behavior therapy (DBT), a type of therapy developed by Marsha Linehan (1993) that combines mindfulness with skills to manage intense feelings and behaviors—activities 10, 11, 13–18, 24–27, 28, 35, 37, 39

3. Mindfulness-based stress reduction (Stahl and Goldstein 2010), which includes specific mindfulness practices that can help reduce tension, anger, and reactivity—activities 7–9, 12, 21–23, 30–33, 38, 40–41, 43, 46

The forty-six numbered activities include a combination of exercises to do in the workbook and skills to practice in the real world. Guided mindfulness practices and meditations are a major part of the book, and we have provided links to several guided meditation recordings you can download. We encourage you to practice these as regularly as possible; put them on your smartphone so you can use them whenever and wherever. There are additional online materials to support your learning. Please see the back of this book for instructions on accessing these recordings and materials, which are available at http://www.newharbinger.com/29163.

Several activities ask you to write personal reflections. Other sections ask you to track your progress. We encourage you to keep a journal for these purposes; journaling can be a very effective way to follow your own inner and outward growth.

Our goal is to give you the best set of tools possible to understand where your anger comes from, handle out-of-control feelings and actions, and ultimately feel happier and more at peace with yourself and others. We are trying to combat years of destructive patterns and provide concentrated practice of new behaviors, training your brain to (a) be mindful of triggers, (b) identify thoughts, feelings, and beliefs, (c) assess the safest option, and (d) use the power of choice to select a response. This is a lot. To be effective, this effort needs to be constant and clear.

Our wish is for you to find the relief and happiness you deserve.

Our hope is that you give it a try.

—Mark Purcell, MEd, PsyD

—Jason Murphy Pedulla, MA, MFTI

the story of two wolves

We congratulate you on taking the first step toward managing your anger and share this story as an inspiration.

One evening, an old Cherokee man told his grandson about a battle that goes on inside all people. He said, "My son, the battle is between two 'wolves' inside us all.

"One is Bad. It is anger, envy, jealousy, sorrow, regret, greed, arrogance, self-pity, guilt, resentment, inferiority, lies, false pride, superiority, and ego.

"The other is Good. It is joy, peace, love, hope, serenity, humility, kindness, benevolence, empathy, generosity, truth, compassion, and faith."

The grandson thought for a minute and then asked his grandfather, "Which wolf wins?"

The old Cherokee man simply replied, "The one you feed."

Feed the good "wolf"!

Jason's Story

When I was sixteen, I was sent to a shrink. Well, he was a psychologist, and I was sent there because I was told I had an anger problem. *Anger isn't my problem*, I thought. *You're my problem.* You being the schools and the teachers who constantly ridiculed me and made me feel less than. You being the adults in my life who didn't know how to talk to me. I felt everyone was pointing the finger at me and saying I was the problem.

I had been caught vandalizing (which really meant breaking stuff) and put on probation. So I go to see this guy, Dr. Dass. I had met him before, in his office at school or in juvenile hall, I can't remember which. I do remember going into his office and seeing lots of rocks and crystals. Right away, I was taken by their differences.

He said, "You like stones?"

"They're all right," I said, not wanting to let him know I thought they were really cool.

He said, "I collect them. Most of these are from the places I've traveled. They each carry a good memory."

I thought, *I've never been anywhere. And I don't have a good memory of anything.*

Later, Dr. Dass talked with me about how sometimes we collect the stones of our lives. Our experiences—what happened to us or around us when we were young, the hurts and mistreatments—can be like stones we pick up along the way. He explained that not all stones are negative. But some of the hurts and mistreatments can feel the heaviest.

I thought about it and agreed that I had been carrying around some stones: anger, resentment, hurt.

Dr. Dass talked about how if we don't learn to let these stones go they just continue to weigh us down. If we hold on to these experiences, they start to harden into our view of the world.

I admitted silently that I didn't think very much of the world. And when I was told that I was angry, I just believed I was just an angry person and couldn't change.

One day, Dr. Dass talked to me about a way he had learned to let go of some of his negative stones. He called it self-hypnosis and asked if I was willing to give it a try.

I said sure, why not. But I have to admit I was skeptical. Over time I had come to trust Dr. Dass, but he was still an adult and a shrink.

I gave it a try. The process was simple. We sat outside in the garden behind his office, and he directed me to simply follow my breath, to open to the sounds around me and listen. Breathe in, knowing that I'm breathing in; breathe out, knowing that I'm breathing out. I closed my eyes and did just that. He then directed me to just allow thoughts and sounds to move through the mind, like clouds through the sky.

At first this was hard to do. My thoughts raced, my body was agitated. But after a few minutes of just relaxing into the breath and the body, I started to feel a bit calmer. For a few moments on that day, I learned what it meant to be at peace with myself.

Learning to observe thoughts and sounds helped me feel less stressed and, to tell the truth, I kind of felt like I was high, a natural high. After a few minutes, I would get distracted and start thinking, *This is stupid* or *I'm bored*. But Dr. Dass would just direct me back to my breath and start again.

I'd like to be able to tell you that was it, that I never felt anger or frustration again, but that's not the way it works. It has taken many years of practicing what I now know as mindfulness meditation. But that first day I can honestly say I felt some relief from my thoughts, from my judgments.

That first day, Dr. Dass taught me a powerful lesson about how I could change my own reality. And this tool is one I have held on to for many years and have worked hard to develop. To not only find relief from my habitual reactions of anger but also to learn ways to cope with life's problems and let go of the stones that have weighed down my hopes and dreams. It has taken work, action on my part. But that day, I realized that things can change, and I will always be grateful for Dr. Dass for his help and understanding.

I hope you find this same tool helpful.

—Jason Murphy Pedulla, MA, MFTI

understanding your anger patterns

Why do I get so angry? Where did this rage come from? How come I can't control myself? These might be some of the questions you ask yourself. Anger is a powerful and complex emotion. Like a tree's roots, the roots of anger can go very deep and spread in several different directions. This chapter will explain some of the causes for anger and aggression and ask you to investigate the roots of your own anger.

People don't usually have problems with what you *feel*, they have problems with what you *do*. So many anger-management strategies fail because all the attention is on making you change what you do: arguing, fighting, out-of-control behaviors. If people knew all the thoughts and feelings you were experiencing underneath your actions, they would probably be more understanding, but no one (including you sometimes) has all that knowledge. This book is about change. But to change what is happening on the outside, we need to look deeply at what is happening on the inside.

1 what's your anger style?

Not everyone fits into one anger style, but knowing more about the different styles can help you better understand your unique pattern for handling anger. Learning about the anger style you tend to rely on can be the first step toward self-understanding and change.

exercise: identifying your anger style

1.	I try to never get angry.	Yes	No
2.	I get really nervous when others are angry.	Yes	No
3.	I feel I'm doing something bad when I get angry.	Yes	No
4.	I often tell people I'll do what they want, but then I forget.	Yes	No
5.	I frequently say things like "Yeah, but ..." and "I'll do it later."	Yes	No
6.	People tell me I must be angry but I'm not sure why.	Yes	No
7.	I get mad at myself a lot.	Yes	No
8.	I bottle up my anger and then get headaches, stiff necks, stomachaches, or other physical symptoms.	Yes	No
9.	I frequently call myself ugly names like "dummy" or "selfish."	Yes	No
10.	My anger comes on really fast.	Yes	No
11.	I act before I think when I get angry.	Yes	No
12.	My anger goes away very quickly.	Yes	No
13.	I get very angry when people criticize me.	Yes	No
14.	People say I'm easily hurt and oversensitive.	Yes	No
15.	I get angry easily when I feel bad about myself.	Yes	No
16.	I get mad in order to get what I want.	Yes	No
17.	I try to scare others with my anger.	Yes	No
18.	I sometimes pretend to be angry when I'm not.	Yes	No

19.	Sometimes I get angry just for the excitement or action.	Yes	No
20.	I like the strong feelings that come with my anger.	Yes	No
21.	Sometimes when I'm bored I start arguments or pick fights.	Yes	No
22.	I seem to get angry all the time.	Yes	No
23.	My anger feels like a bad habit I have trouble breaking.	Yes	No
24.	I get mad without thinking—it feels automatic.	Yes	No
25.	I get jealous a lot, even when there is no reason.	Yes	No
26.	I don't trust people very much.	Yes	No
27.	Sometimes it feels like people are out to get me.	Yes	No
28.	I become very angry when I defend my beliefs and opinions.	Yes	No
29.	I often feel outraged about what others try to get away with.	Yes	No
30.	I always know I'm right in an argument.	Yes	No
31.	I hang on to my anger for a long time.	Yes	No
32.	I have a hard time forgiving people.	Yes	No
33.	I hate people for what they've done to me.	Yes	No

Now that you have completed this quiz, let's take a look at which anger style you tend to rely on. The questions are broken into sets of three. Each set relates to one of eleven anger styles that fall into three groups: masked, explosive, and chronic. Within a set, two "Yes" answers indicate an anger style you rely on often; three "Yes" answers suggest a style you use frequently and perhaps all the time.

In addition to the material that follows, you can learn more about these anger styles at http://www.newharbinger.com/29163. For each style, the online material includes a detailed description, an illustrative story, a description of the problems that may result, and additional tips for what to work on. See the back of this book for instructions on downloading this material.

masked anger

Questions 1–9 relate to masked anger. People who rely on this style are mostly unaware or unaccepting of their anger. They are afraid to upset others, and keep anger hidden. There are three types of masked anger:

1. People pleasing (questions 1–3)

   People pleasers believe that anger is bad, scary, or useless. They try to keep everyone satisfied and avoid anger at all costs.

2. Sneaky (4–6)

   Anger is expressed indirectly by frustrating others through inaction. These people have trouble saying no, so they express anger through sarcasm, gossip, and other passive-aggressive ways.

3. Self-blaming (7–9)

   These people believe it is better to blame yourself than to directly express your feelings. Taking the blame for everything that goes wrong results in anger and can cause low self-esteem or depression.

To free yourself from masked anger, work on

- realizing that it's okay to be angry, to hear and express disagreement;

- expressing your anger so that it doesn't come out in unhealthy ways;

- being direct about what you are feeling without worrying about whether you will lose the relationship.

These activities can help you with masked anger: 2–5, 10–12, 16–19, 34–36, 42–45.

explosive anger

Questions 10–21 relate to explosive anger styles. People who rely on this anger pattern tend to lose control of their anger easily and at times can hurt others. There are four types of this style:

1. Volcanic (questions 10–12)

    Intense anger comes on suddenly and feels out of control. There is some relief after releasing bottled-up rage. Afterward, the person feels bad.

2. Defensive (13–15)

    Defensive anger occurs in people who are very sensitive. The slightest comment feels like an attack on the person, not just the behavior. The person becomes defensive and turns blame around, and is often more angry than the other person.

3. Intimidating (16–18)

    Anger is used to intimidate others. Once these people get what they want, their anger goes away quickly.

4. Raging (19–21)

    These people get a rush out of anger. They like the surge of energy and drama.

To free yourself from explosive anger, work on

-   noticing early signs of anger and developing body awareness to calm physical reactions;

-   expressing how you feel instead of bottling it up;

-   not taking everything as a personal attack;

-   not using your anger to get your way, scare others, or get a rush. In the long run it is not worth it; your relationships will suffer.

These activities can help you with explosive anger: 3–6, 10–18, 19–27, 29–30, 35–39, 42–45.

chronic anger

Questions 22–33 relate to the chronic anger style. People who have developed this pattern have made anger part of their lifestyle. There are four types of chronic anger:

1. Grumpy (questions 22–24)

    These people focus on what is wrong with everything. They see the bad in others, not the good. Life often feels like a burden. Depression may be involved in this type of anger.

2. Suspicious (25–27)

    These people have trouble trusting others and are on guard most of the time. It feels safer to expect the worst from others.

3. Moral (28–30)

    Anger is justified because it is morally "right." It is the job of these people to be sure that others follow rules, and they get angry when others don't see things their way.

4. Vengeful (31–33)

    These people have trouble forgiving. It is hard for them to let go of past hurts. There are people they hate, and they try to make others pay for what was done wrong to them.

To free yourself from chronic anger, work on

- seeing the good in others;

- engaging in fun and positive activities;

- learning to trust and starting off with the belief that people have good intentions;

- learning to be flexible and open to the opinions of others;

- letting go of past hurts for the sake of your own happiness.

These activities can help you with chronic anger: 2–6, 10–12, 14–21, 24–30, 34–46.

beneath the surface 2

Did you know that icebergs show only one-ninth of their mass above water? The other eight-ninths are hidden beneath the surface. People can be the same way. We often show a small part of ourselves to the outside world and keep the rest hidden, sometimes even from ourselves. We may act strong or intimidating on the outside, but underneath we might feel afraid. Or we may appear confident and popular, but underneath we might be afraid of what others think about us, or terrified of failing.

exercise: above and below

In the space below, write down what you show others on the surface. Complete the next sentences with what you really think and feel beneath the surface. Include the messages you heard from others that may have caused you to feel that way. Finally, think of something you can do to share what is below the surface: the inner experience you keep from others.

To others, I seem

_____

Underneath the surface, I think I am

_____

Underneath, I really feel

_____

In the past, I was told or I experienced

_____

To share this inner experience with someone else, I can

_____

3 feeling safe

Why do anger and fear feel so much stronger in our bodies than pleasant emotions like happiness or calmness? It's because they evoke an emergency alarm system known as the fight-or-flight response, a survival instinct we share with most living creatures. When we sense danger, our bodies automatically try to protect us by releasing hormones that provide a burst of energy. We become highly sensitive to our surroundings. Our bodies get primed for action, and our more advanced thought processes go offline.

This response is important when there is a real threat to our survival. At those times, we need to react fast. But what if there is no immediate threat? If we are in fight-or-flight mode, we end up reacting before we have really thought through the best way to handle a situation.

Fear is often the emotion buried beneath our anger. There are all kinds of fears you might try to avoid or mask with your anger. Your internal fears may trigger your fight-or-flight alarm, even when they aren't threats to your physical safety. Most fights do not start because of real threats.

exercise: common fears and threats

Below is a list of common fears and threats people experience. Check the ones you have the strongest reactions to.

I am afraid of…	I react most strongly to threats against…
☐ failure	☐ my pride—respect from others
☐ rejection	☐ my people—those close to me
☐ being alone or abandoned	☐ my stuff—possessions, space
☐ being hurt emotionally	☐ my goals—what I want to do

None of these fears present an immediate threat to your physical safety. They come from your own worries and interpretations and can put you into fight-or-flight mode. The problem is that fighting or running will not make these kinds of threats go away. Say you try to run from your fear of rejection by avoiding any close relationships. The fear will not go away and will likely get worse. Or you try to fight away threats to your pride. You could fight every person you think threatens your respect. Will that threat ever go away? No, it will likely grow until you are on guard against everyone.

The fight-or-flight alarm system does not work for fears that come from our inner feelings and insecurities. If anything, acting on primitive fear instincts rather than using our minds makes situations worse, so calming down this highly sensitive alarm system is a very important skill.

informal practice: I am safe

Use this simple technique to remind your body that you are not in immediate danger.

- First ask yourself, *Am I safe from immediate physical harm?* (If the answer is no, follow your flight instincts and get someplace safe.)

- Take in a deep, slow breath, and say to yourself, *I am safe.* You can also place your hand over your heart, which helps calm the nervous system. Remind yourself that whatever is upsetting you is not threatening your physical safety.

- When you exhale, try to release any tension you feel in your body.

- Repeat.

Continue this simple exercise until you feel your body come out of the high-alert mode and back to a state of regular ease.

the seeds of anger 4

You weren't born angry. None of us were. But anger and aggression are all around us. Anger can be like a seed planted inside of us. What started as something forced on us can grow within us until it becomes who we are.

Nick's Story: Angry Habits

Nick is an angry kid. He walks around school kicking trash cans. He gets into fights. He has a couple of friends who are similar to him, and sometimes they're even mean to each other, but mostly they just cause havoc with other kids. Nick gets a lot of negative attention from teachers and principals, and he's always in trouble.

The seeds of anger had been planted inside Nick and that anger grew and spread to others, reinforcing the perception that he was an angry person. Nick would say, "This is just the way I am. Deal with it." But here's the other side of the story.

Nick's Other Story: The Seeds of Anger

At home Nick is quiet, well-mannered, and respectful. At least it seems that way. He frequently hears his parents argue loudly. His older brother takes a lot of abuse from their dad, some physical. Nick feels in constant threat of being attacked verbally or physically. Nick is often angry at his father for being abusive and mean. He is angry at his mother for sticking around and taking the abuse. He is scared for his brother. Their dad rules the house with an iron fist, and Nick feels powerless. At school Nick can release some of this anger, so he does.

exercise: the seeds of anger

Here are some examples of the seeds of anger many teens experience. Mark the ones that are part of your life. Add some of your own.

☐   Violence in school   ☐   Violent video games or movies

☐   Conflict at home   ☐   Put-downs and verbal abuse

☐   Friends who fight   ☐   Alcohol or drugs

☐   Being bullied   ☐   _____

☐   Feeling abandoned   ☐   _____

☐   Neighborhood violence   ☐   _____

It can be difficult to think of painful experiences from our past. We would rather lock them away and try to forget about them. But our bodies and brains remember these experiences, often in that primitive part where our fight-or-flight responses are stored. This means that sometimes we react to current situations with the same intense feelings we had long ago, when we felt scared, angry, or overwhelmed. This can happen very fast and without our totally making the connection. But it's one reason why we can suddenly feel really upset and overwhelmed by a situation that may not seem to be a big deal to someone else.

informal practice: remembering past hurts and mistreatments

Find a quiet place that is comfortable for you. Take a few quiet moments, and try to think of past painful experiences: times when you felt scared or angry or alone, or past situations that caused you emotional or physical pain. To help get them outside your thoughts and bodily reactions, you may want to write down your memories in your journal. This practice may be difficult, so be compassionate toward yourself and take breaks when you need to.

Practice the mindfulness skill *I Am Safe* from the activity Feeling Safe. Remind yourself, *Then is not now.*

5 the cycle of anger

We can get into the habit of seeing threats and danger everywhere. Anger and hatred can become the feelings that dominate our emotions, feeding into a cycle of anger, a pattern that is difficult to escape. This pattern also leads to what is called a self-fulfilling prophecy, which means we end up creating a negative reality that supports the negative way we view ourselves and others. If you are focused on anger, you will create a violent life around you.

Using Nick's story from Actvity 4 as an example, here is how the cycle of anger works.

Negative self-view—the negative thoughts we say to ourselves (often learned from others)

Nick, learning from things said by his father, thinks, *Everyone hates me and is out to get me.*

External triggering event—something that happens and causes our reactions

A classmate accidentally bumps Nick in school.

Internal trigger—an intense negative emotional reaction to the event

Nick thinks, *He's messing with me.*

Angry behavior—an impulsive reaction to the event

Nick gets in his classmate's face and throws him against the lockers.

Response from adults—rejection, disappointment, and possibly punishment

Nick gets suspended from school and yelled at by his parents.

Response from peers—rejection, fear, and avoidance

Nick's classmates stay away from him because he is mean and out of control.

Self-fulfilling prophecy—reality begins to match the negative self-view

Nick gets a bad reputation with teachers, his parents are angry, and his classmates avoid him, confirming Nick's belief that everyone hates him.

exercise: breaking angry habits

Breaking the cycle of anger can be very difficult. Being aware of its happening is the first step. Write down the negative messages you say about yourself, or negative ways you believe others may view you; here again, examples based on Nick's story have been provided. Being aware of the negative messages you tell yourself can help you notice when they may be distorting your view of situations.

1. Turn self-messages from negative to positive.

    Nick: *Not everyone hates me. I have friends who like me. My mom and grandma like me too.*

    I think that others don't like me because _____

    When I am down, I think that I am _____

    To turn these self-messages positive, I can think _____

2. Recognize your triggers.

    Nick: *When someone gets in my space, I think they're threatening me, but maybe they aren't. I should figure out what someone else's intention is before I assume that person is against me.*

    What things usually trigger your anger?

    _____

    _____

3. Focus on the best in others, not the worst. Assume that other people have good intentions. Notice when you are on guard and assuming others are out to get you.

    Nick: *Instead of assuming others are trying to be mean to me, I'll focus on their being positive toward me. I'll think to myself,* They mean well *instead of* They want to hurt me.

4. Don't paint your own bad picture.

    Notice whether you are creating a self-fulfilling prophecy. If you realize you
    are, you can stop believing in the self-defeating thoughts that may be starting to
    become your own reality. You have the power to create a positive self-fulfilling
    prophecy also, using your own good intentions and actions.

    Nick: *I believe I am a good person; I will behave like a good person; and others will
    notice that I am a good person.*

power struggles 6

How often does it feel like everyone is against you? The battle over control is one of the biggest causes of anger and aggressive behavior, and power struggles are one of the biggest sources of conflict between youth and parents. Power plays into anger problems in different ways.

For example, when you have very little control over a situation, you feel powerless. *Powerlessness* is the curse of being an adolescent, wanting to make your own decisions but having to follow all these adult rules that seem stupid. Feeling powerless day after day can be a breeding ground for anger.

Abuse of power, the use of power to control others, is another example. You may feel powerless in one part of your life, so you abuse power in another. It's a way to get back at someone else for how you have been made to feel.

Anger habits often develop from unhealthy struggles for power. You may have learned—from home, from friends—that threatening others lets you get what you want. You may be able to control your parents with the threat of out-of-control behavior, like violence or meltdowns. But is this really the type of relationship you want? Teachers, friends, and others may not cave so easily. In fact, they'll probably avoid you. In the short run, abusing power can give you control over others. In the long run, it will leave you miserable and alone.

Empowerment is the balanced sense of power that comes from within. You don't feel powerless, and you aren't abusing power over others. Instead you have a healthy self-confidence that enables you to achieve what you hope to achieve, and not at the expense of others. Empowerment is the only kind of power that actually feels good— for you and others.

exercise: power struggles

For each of the stories below, decide whether the person is (a) feeling powerless, (b) abusing power, or (c) acting empowered. After each story, write down the letter that matches.

Ashley

Ashley loves her boyfriend Luke. But Luke wants Ashley with him all the time. He makes her feel bad when she spends time with friends or her family. Recently, he convinced her to skip tutoring after school to be with him. He said that if she didn't spend time with him she would be a horrible girlfriend, and he threatened to break up with her.

Ashley is _____

At home, Ashley can be really mean to her family. She bullies her little sister. When her parents found out that Ashley had skipped tutoring, they tried to ground her. She exploded, saying she hated them and threatening to hurt herself if they kept her prisoner.

Ashley is _____

Jasmine

Jasmine's mom is really overprotective. She is always afraid something bad will happen, so she never lets Jasmine go out without supervision. Her mom reads her texts and Facebook. Jasmine is always grounded for the smallest things. She is so angry that she has considered running away.

Jasmine is _____

Jasmine talks to her school counselor about the situation at home, and the counselor arranges family therapy for Jasmine and her mom. The counselor helps Jasmine express her feelings and helps her mom deal with her own anxiety. Although it is difficult, Jasmine and her mom are able to negotiate rules they can both live with.

Jasmine is _____

Lucas

Lucas has some learning difficulties; school has always been hard for him. Other kids also pick on him. He feels like he is dumb and will never get it.

Lucas is _____

Lucas starts talking back to his teachers and getting into fights with other kids. He acts like school doesn't matter, and as if he believes that no one can make him do anything.

Lucas is _____

exercise: being empowered

During the next week, try to notice when you get into power struggles.

What situations make you feel powerless?

_____

_____

_____

_____

How do you threaten others to gain power and control (physical aggression, emotional meltdowns, verbally)?

_____

_____

_____

_____

How can you approach these situations from a place of empowerment and self-confidence, where you feel better, but not at the expense of others?

_____

_____

_____

_____

the power of mindfulness

We often do not recognize what is happening inside of us when we are angry. We are focusing our attention on what is going wrong out there. We also do not stick with what we are experiencing. Instead we do whatever we can to get rid of that feeling—scream, lash out, avoid.

How many times have you wished you could take back something you did or said when you felt out of control with anger? How many times have you reacted first and felt bad later? Imagine if you could hit a pause button during every fight, then take your time to decide what the best action might be. With practice, mindfulness can become your pause button.

In the most basic way, mindfulness is about focusing your attention on two fundamental questions:

1. *What is happening right now inside me?*

   Ask yourself these questions right now: What are you feeling in your body—in this moment? What are you thinking—in this moment? What are all the feelings you are experiencing—in this moment? The key is to keep your awareness anchored to *right now.* This is mindful awareness.

2. *Can I stick with my experience right now?*

   Pay attention to what is happening right now without avoiding it or judging it. Can you keep your full attention focused on what you are experiencing in this moment, without trying to get rid of it?

If you can ask yourself these two questions throughout your day, you will be practicing mindfulness. You will develop more self-awareness and self-control.

The practice of mindfulness means learning to trust what you are actually experiencing. It takes patience and a willingness to describe what is happening without judgment. Regular practice of mindfulness is a simple and realistic way to develop the power of open awareness. This power can become stronger than the strength of your own negative habits.

Mindfulness practice can be done in two ways: formal and informal. Formal practice involves sitting in a quiet place and having a structured time of mindfulness; for example, a guided meditation. Informal practices are mindfulness techniques you can use in the moment, any time throughout the day—for example, stopping to take a breath and observe before you proceed. We will let you know which is which throughout this workbook.

mindful check-in 7

Mindfulness can be used like a pause button in your crazy day. Take a few minutes to just be. Take a break from your worries about the future or regrets about the past. Stop and observe. What are you experiencing in your body, thinking in your mind, and feeling in your heart? Try to do this mindful check-in a few times a day to build your self-awareness.

formal practice: mindful check-in

The written instructions below are a simplified version of the full guided meditation that can be downloaded at http://www.newharbinger.com/29163. We recommend that you listen to the audio recording to get the full benefits of this meditation. Start with these basic steps. Pause for about five breaths between each step.

- Take a few moments to be still.

- Feel into your body and mind. Allow any waves of thought, feelings, or body sensations to just be.

- Try to *be* in the moment instead of trying to *do* something.

- Turn your attention inward. Notice changing sensations, feelings, and thoughts. Pause for a few breaths.

- Congratulate yourself for doing this practice.

8 self-reflection

Find a quiet place where you will be free from distractions for five to ten minutes. For each statement, take a minute or two to let it sink in. Allow your thoughts and emotions to emerge on their own in response to the statement.

formal practice: self-reflection

First, read each statement, and pause for a minute or two after each one, to direct your attention inward. The words in parentheses are there to help guide your attention to the experience.

If you really knew me, you'd know...

(Notice sensations in your body. Notice thoughts, words, or images that enter your mind. Notice emotions that come to the surface.)

_____

_____

_____

I cause my own suffering by...

(Allow yourself to experience any shift in how you feel. Notice any images or thoughts. Notice any difference in your body. Try not to judge yourself. Just notice what comes to mind and body.)

_____

_____

_____

I can increase my happiness by…

(Allow any thoughts or images to enter awareness. Bring awareness to any shift in feelings and sensations. Do you feel lighter or more hopeful? Just let the thoughts, feelings, and sensations emerge.)

_____

_____

_____

Congratulate yourself for taking this time to look inward at yourself. Now, in the space provided, write down what came up for you in response to each step.

9 breathing in the moment

We may be caught up in what happened a while ago or worrying about what is coming up. With our minds in the future or past, we are missing the opportunity to connect to the present. Ground yourself to this moment, which is all you really have. This simple, yet powerful practice will connect you to the present by following the rhythm of your breath.

formal practice: breathing in the moment

The written instructions below are a simplified version of the full guided meditation that can be downloaded at http://www.newharbinger.com/29163. We recommend that you listen to the audio recording to get the full benefits of this meditation.

Start with these basic steps. Pause for about five breaths between each step.

- Get into a comfortable position. Connect to the body sitting; feel the places of contact with the chair and the floor.

- Connect with your breath. Breathe normally. Follow the rise and fall of the breath.

- Notice the sensation of breath at the tip of the nose. Notice the coolness of the in-breath and the warmth of the out-breath. As you breathe in, think, *In*. As you breathe out, think, *Out*.

- If your attention wanders away from the breath, notice that it is wandering. Gently bring attention back to the breath.

- Use the breath as an anchor to keep connected to the moment.

- Say to yourself, *Breathing in, I calm my mind. Breathing out, I relax my body.*

- Repeat, *Breathing in, calm; breathing out, relax.*

- With each breath, go deeper into the present moment.

- Gently allow your eyes to open and slowly begin to move your body.

- Congratulate yourself for taking this time to just be.

trusting your wise mind 10

Our problems often occur in the interval between an event and our reaction. If you have problems with anger, you may feel that you have very little control over what you do in response to an upsetting situation. Often this feeling arises because you are not allowing enough space between what happens to upset you and how you react. You may not be fully aware of the thoughts, feelings, and sensations that inform how you respond.

What mindfulness can do is give you a pause between the event and the reaction. With practice, you can be the mindful observer of what is happening inside you. This is trusting your wise mind.

Sophia's Story: Emotional Mind and Wise Mind

Sophia's best friend, Olivia, went to the movies with Danielle, a girl Sophia hates, and didn't tell Sophia. When Sophia first finds out, she is furious and her heart pounds. She can't believe Olivia would betray her like that. These thoughts and feelings come over her all at once. Her first urge is to text Olivia and tell her what a terrible friend she is.

But Sophia remembers her mindfulness practice and tries to rely on her wise mind instead of acting on her intense feelings and impulsive urges. Using mindfulness, Sophia is able to observe her thoughts, feelings, and bodily sensations without getting swept up in them.

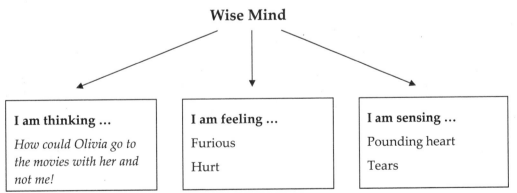

Wise Mind

I am thinking …	**I am feeling …**	**I am sensing …**
How could Olivia go to the movies with her and not me!	Furious Hurt	Pounding heart Tears

With space between the upsetting event and her reaction, Sophia's mindful response is to call Olivia and ask why she didn't tell her about the movies. Sophia expresses that she felt hurt, and the two work it out.

informal practice: trust your wise mind

During the next week, practice using your wise mind. First, try this mindfulness practice during calm situations. Then try to use it during more stressful interactions. Get into your wise mind and ask yourself:

- *What is happening in my body right now?*

- *What am I thinking right now?*

- *What am I feeling right now?*

Write down your observations in your journal.

acceptance and change 11

How often do you get angry because of how unfair things are? Well, we have some bad news—sometimes life is unfair. And getting angry about it can make it worse. Acceptance and change are two very important principles for dealing with anger (and are important to DBT skills and mindfulness). Here is a saying used by many people to help them figure this out:

Grant me the serenity to accept the things I cannot change, the courage to change the things I can, and the wisdom to know the difference.

The nonacceptance version would read:

I am angry about the things I cannot change. Because I am hurt and this feels unfair, I refuse to do the things I can do to change.

Anger often comes from being unable to accept the painful parts of life: past hurts, present struggles, or future fears. Practicing acceptance does not mean giving up. Instead, it is about accepting the reality of things. Some things you do have control over, others you may not. Acceptance can keep you from getting angry about situations you cannot change. If nothing can be done, practice acceptance. Otherwise, you may make things worse by trying to avoid the reality of the situation.

Ethan's Story: What Do I Need to Accept?

Ethan has learning difficulties that make school hard for him. He may need to work harder at school than other kids. Sometimes, no matter how hard he tries, he may not get an A. This is really hard to accept without getting mad or giving up. But if he can accept this reality, he can figure out how to best handle it.

Ethan is angry because his problems seem unfair, and maybe they are. But getting angry at the world for being unfair isn't making anything better. If Ethan practices acceptance of things he cannot change, then he can direct his energy toward doing some of the things that might make a difference.

Ethan's Story Rewritten: What Can I Change?

Ethan can change his attitude and focus on his successes instead of failures. He can change how he thinks of himself—like telling himself, I'm trying my best *instead of* I'm stupid. *He can change what he does—like asking for help or trying his best instead of acting like he doesn't care.*

exercise: willful or willing?

When you are willful, you refuse to accept things the way they are. Willful people try to use willpower to force things to be the way they feel they should be, rather than accepting them the way they are. Handling life from a willful place is like being a boulder, smashing through things until you bang up against something bigger. Mark the ways that you are willful when things do not go your way.

☐ Refusing to accept the present situation	☐ Trying to "fix" everything	
☐ Acting stubborn	☐ Giving up	
☐ Complaining	☐ Threatening	

When you practice willingness, you accept life on its terms. Willingness may not always fix a situation, but it keeps us from getting angrier and making it worse. When we are willing, there is more opportunity for change. Handling life from a willing place is like being a river, flowing through and around obstacles that block your way. Check off the ways to be willing that you use (or would like to try in the next week).

☐ Negotiating	☐ Listening to the "other side"	
☐ Accepting what is	☐ Being flexible	
☐ Living life on life's terms	☐ Being open	
☐ Trying your best	☐ Cooperating instead of competing	

During the next week, notice when you are being willful and try to let go, to be flexible. Practice being willing in difficult situations. See if you notice a difference in how people relate to you and how things work out.

12 self-acceptance

Self-acceptance is the most important (and often most difficult) place to start practicing acceptance. In this mindfulness practice, create a sense of self-compassion by imagining how you would support a close friend in your situation. What could you say to be comforting?

Take a few moments to reflect on this. Think of what you might say to your friend. (Here's a start: *You are safe. You are good. You deserve to be happy and free from suffering.*)

Now consider some of the ways that you too have felt sad, unhappy, or angry. Offer words of compassion that are similar to what you would offer your friend. (Here's a start: *I am safe. I am good. I deserve to be happy and free from suffering.*)

formal practice: self-acceptance

Notice what happens in your body and mind as you offer these expressions of kindness to yourself. What comes up for you in your thoughts, feelings, and sensations? Turn your awareness to the painful places in you (feelings, memories, or body sensations). Say to yourself, *I care for this suffering.* Try to feel deeply into your suffering, and investigate the way you would feel toward a friend going through similar pain and suffering.

Try to breathe into the tight places in your body, inviting a little more tension to release each time you exhale. You may find unkind thoughts arising (toward yourself and others). Simply allow the negative thoughts to come and go. Know that these angry, unkind thoughts likely arise from fear. Like all sensations, these thoughts and feelings will pass like clouds drifting through the sky, coming and going. Turn your compassion toward any hurt feelings or painful memories that may have been stirred up. Repeat again to yourself, *I care for this suffering.*

Close by practicing mindful breathing for five to ten minutes. Offer yourself gratitude and congratulations for giving yourself this gift of mindfulness and self-compassion.

preparing to change

Change is hard, very hard. If it were easy, we would all do the "right" things for ourselves. We can get into habits of thinking about things the same way and reacting to situations the same way. You may tell yourself that you want things to be different, but the same things happen over and over. The first step to making a change in your life is to notice the patterns that lead you down the same road to the same unhappy destination. This poem describes the challenge to change.

Autobiography in Five Short Chapters[*]

Chapter One

I walk down the street.
> There is a deep hole in the sidewalk.
> I fall in.
> I am lost ... I am helpless.
>> It isn't my fault.
It takes forever to find a way out.

Chapter Two

I walk down the same street.
> There is a deep hole in the sidewalk.
> I pretend I don't see it.
> I fall in again.
I can't believe I am in this same place.
> But, it isn't my fault.
It still takes a long time to get out.

Chapter Three

I walk down the same street.
    There is a deep hole in the sidewalk.
    I *see* it is there.
    I still fall in ... it's a habit ... but,
        my eyes are open.
        I know where I am.
  It is *my* fault.
  I get out immediately.

Chapter Four

I walk down the same street.
    There is a deep hole in the sidewalk.
    I walk around it.

Chapter Five

I walk down another street.

How often have you told yourself, *I wouldn't get so angry if ...*? Each of us would complete that sentence differently. The problem with blaming other people and situations for our anger is that we have very little control over them. The only person you can truly change is yourself. So if you really want to cope with your anger differently, you have to be willing to take a serious look at yourself. Stop hoping that the people and situations out there will change, and begin the difficult job of looking inward. Find a new path to follow.

A similar DBT principle is this: *You may not have caused your problems, but you are responsible for what you do about them.* Anger often comes from a place of pain and hurt. But if you stay angry at the people and situations that caused the pain, you will never get free. You need to make the decision for yourself if you want to change your life. That change starts with you. Essentially, there are only five different ways that you can handle any problem. Which one do you choose most often?

1. Fix the problem.

   If there is a solution to the problem, use your wise mind to solve the problem.

2. Change your attitude.

   Some situations you view as a problem may not be so bad if you change your perspective about them.

3. Accept the situation.

   Some problems cannot be solved and may still leave you feeling bad. In these situations, work on acceptance, then let the problem go. Redirect your attention to other positive activities.

4. Stay miserable.

   If you cannot solve a problem, and you refuse to accept it or change your attitude, then you are choosing to stay miserable. At any point, you can choose to accept things as they are, and you are then free to let go of staying miserable.

5. Make it worse.

   When your anger gets the best of you, you may impulsively do things that make the situation even worse. This pattern can quickly get out of control. What started as a small disagreement can escalate into a huge problem.

13 how do you cope with anger?

We experience a range of feelings in different situations—excitement, happiness, pain, or fear. We also develop patterns for what we do to handle these different feelings. Let's call that coping. Some of these ways to cope can be healthy, like laughing when we are happy. At other times, we react to intense feelings with unhealthy coping strategies, like checking out with the help of drugs when we're upset, or fighting when we feel criticized. Learning to identify our feelings and how we cope with them can be the first step toward making better choices for ourselves.

Angela's Story: Fighting to Cope with Pain

When Angela was thirteen, her parents divorced. She had to move with her mom to a new neighborhood. The kids in her new school are tough. She hates school and doesn't feel she can talk to her parents about it. One group of girls at school called Angela mean names and got in her face. She didn't know how to make it stop, and she bottled up her feelings. The insults and horrible feelings built up until she suddenly exploded at her mom. She screamed at her and even tried to hit her. Then she started to explode at school. She picked on the girls who were weaker than her. Angela has become one of the mean girls and has even started to hang out with them. She feels alone and angry most of the time, always looking for someone to fight. She never wanted to be this way, but it just happened over time.

Like Angela, you may have times when your life feels out of control. The outside world may be threatening. Inside, your feelings may be a jumbled mess of pain and anger. And the way you react to all of this may feel out of control. The ways you "cope"—like Angela's exploding—or survive these upsetting situations and feelings may lead to more intense feelings and more craziness. This is how unhealthy coping habits can start.

Unhealthy coping habits are the ways we try to make painful feelings go away—like drugs, unhealthy eating, or fighting. They give us short-term relief, but in the long run, they can cause our lives to spin out of control.

exercise: how you cope with anger

The first step to changing this crazy pattern in your life is to figure out which coping strategies are causing you the most problems. Mark the ways you cope when your anger becomes too much to handle. Use the blank lines to add others.

☐ Hitting   ☐ Breaking things   ☐ Sarcasm

☐ Yelling or screaming   ☐ Bullying   ☐ Mocking or teasing

☐ Crying   ☐ Cutting or self-harming   ☐ Provoking

☐ Doing drugs or drinking   ☐ Ignoring or pouting   ☐ Withdrawing

☐ Threatening   ☐ Melting down   ☐ Running away

☐ _____

☐ _____

Identify the three behaviors you believe are most out of control and cause you the most problems:

1. _____

2. _____

3. _____

Try to name the specific emotions you experience before engaging in these behaviors.

_____

_____

How do you feel immediately after engaging in these behaviors?

_____

_____

How do you feel one day after you engage in these behaviors?

_____

_____

You may feel immediate relief after engaging in these coping strategies, but may later regret what you did. During the next week, remind yourself of the long-term consequences of these behaviors. See if you can use this reminder to try to stop yourself from "coping" this way.

the costs and benefits of acting on anger 14

All your behavior serves a purpose. If it didn't, you would simply stop. Maybe your angry behavior gives you what you want, or protects you, or gives you some relief.

To truly change behavior, you have to investigate what you're getting out of it, good and bad. Then you need to figure out what the costs and benefits of changing it would be. It is also important to decide what your goals are, both short-term and long-term, because something that may feel good right now—like hitting a classmate who bothers you—might not help you reach your long-term goals, like graduating from high school. Let's look at the costs and benefits of anger, using Angela from the preceding activity as an example.

Angela's Behavior	Benefits	Costs
Fighting, Threatening	Respect—no one messes with me. Relief—I let my feelings out. Mom gives me my way.	Kids don't like me; they're afraid of me. My feelings are out of control. I don't like myself very much. I'm always on guard. I'm always in trouble.
Not Fighting	Things would be more stable, with less drama. I'd have real friendships. I'd have healthier relationships. There'd be less trouble at school or home.	I might be bullied again. I'd get less "respect." I wouldn't have any relief for painful feelings.

exercise: examining the costs and benefits of your behavior

Take some time to honestly examine the benefits and costs of your current behavior. Then look at the benefits and costs of changing that behavior.

Describe one of your anger-related behaviors. Be as specific as possible.

_____

_____

Benefits: What are the different things you get out of this behavior?

_____

_____

Costs: In what ways does this behavior cause problems for you or others?

_____

_____

Costs of changing: What would you lose if you changed this behavior?

_____

_____

Benefits of changing: What would be the long-term benefits of changing this behavior?

_____

_____

Long-term goals: What are some goals you have for yourself? What steps can you take toward those goals?

_____

_____

_____

_____

_____

_____

15 triggers and anger invitations

We all have certain things that really piss us off and trigger our anger. Triggers can be internal or external. Internal triggers are your inner experiences—thoughts, physical states, or feelings that cause your anger to rise and perhaps finally blow. External triggers are caused by people and situations around you. Your anger can be set off by either of these triggers or both.

Along with triggers, certain types of interactions can feel like an invitation for you to get angry. These are the times when we are triggered by someone and, instead of avoiding the situation, react in a way that causes more conflict and anger. When this happens, we have accepted an anger invitation.

Joshua's Story: Accepting an Anger Invitation

Joshua is anxious at school because he knows he'll be in big trouble when he gets home. Report cards are out, and he's failed two classes. His parents usually ground him when he gets bad grades. When Joshua is walking down the school hall, Blake teases him about his new sneakers. Joshua snaps and shoves Blake.

Joshua's internal trigger is his anxiety about his parents' reaction. His external trigger is Blake's teasing. When the internal trigger collides with the external trigger, Joshua can't control his behavior and lashes out. Instead of walking away, Joshua takes Blake's anger invitation, and his bottled-up worries and frustrations explode into physical aggression.

exercise: what are your triggers?

Here are some external triggers adolescents often deal with. Mark the ones that trigger your anger, and use the blank lines to add others.

☐ Being accused of something you didn't do

☐ Being told no about something you want

☐ Someone getting into your personal space

☐ A person taking your things without asking

☐ Being nagged

☐ Someone getting in your face

☐ Someone making fun of you.

☐ Someone telling lies about you

☐ A person breaking an agreement

☐ Being criticized

☐ _____

☐ _____

Here are some internal triggers that adolescents often experience. Mark the ones that trigger your anger, and use the blank lines to add others.

☐ Feeling nervous or anxious

☐ Being on guard or defensive

☐ Feeling sad or depressed

☐ Feeling frustrated

☐ Being tired

☐ Judging yourself or others

☐ _____

☐ _____

Now think of a time when one of these triggers invited you to anger.

What did the other person do or say that provoked your anger?

_____

_____

_____

What did you tell yourself (thoughts) or feel in your body (sensations) that caused your anger to rise?

_____

_____

_____

What did you do that caused the situation to escalate and your anger to get bigger?

_____

_____

_____

Is there anything you could have done differently to decline this anger invitation?

_____

_____

_____

responding instead of reacting 16

When an event occurs, our minds and bodies respond with thoughts, feelings, and physical sensations. Based on how we interpret these responses, we react. We often experience this as all happening at once, but in reality it is a process. If you learn to rely on your wise mind, you can pause, observe this process, and respond more reasonably instead of reacting impulsively.

David's Story: Reacting to Anger

When David comes home late one day, his parents confront him about skipping school. David denies it, and his dad accuses him of being dishonest. His mom cries, saying that he's going to fail. David is annoyed and defensive. When he tells them to leave him alone, his dad grounds him from going to a concert he wants to attend. Furious, David punches a hole in the wall and storms off to his room. The next day, an attendance officer shows up at David's house. Because of his record of missing school, David is put on in-school suspension.

Let's break down David's thoughts, feelings, and sensations.

Event: His parents yell at David and ground him.

His thoughts: *I wish they would leave me alone; I messed up again; I hate them; I can't miss that concert.*

His feelings: anger, shame, frustration

His physical sensations: pounding heart, clenched fists, tight muscles

David's reaction: He punches a wall and storms off.

What might have happened if David had relied on his wise mind and responded, instead of reacting?

His alternative thoughts: *I messed up, but I don't want to make it worse.*

His alternative feelings: guilt

His alternative physical sensations: pounding heart

David's response: He leaves the argument. Later, he tells his parents why he skipped school and says he won't do that anymore. He's angry about missing the concert, but tells himself he won't decide to act that way again. He'll try to make a wiser choice next time.

informal practice: responding wisely instead of reacting in anger

During the next week, practice mindfully observing your thoughts, feelings, and sensations, and use your journal to write about your experience. After a week, see if you are more aware of this process. Are you better able to choose how to respond instead of reacting impulsively?

CALM log 17

In addition to journaling, keeping track of your behavior patterns can help improve your self-control, so try to fill out a CALM log every day. The title of this log can help you remember to Cope with Anger and Live Mindfully. You can download it at http://www.newharbinger.com/29163 (see the back of this book for instructions).

exercise: keeping a CALM log

Identify the external events or inner thoughts and feelings that triggered your anger.

_____

_____

_____

What did you notice happening in your body and mind?

Thoughts: _____

Feelings: _____

Physical sensations: _____

What was your first urge to react? _____

_____

Rate your urge on a scale from 1–5, with 5 being the most intense: _____

If you acted on your urge, describe what happened. _____

_____

_____

What alternative thoughts, feelings, and physical sensations could you have focused on?

Alternative thoughts: _____

Alternative feelings: _____

Alternative physical sensations: _____

How could you have responded to this event more mindfully? _____

_____

_____

_____

anger mapping 18

You may experience your anger as something that just happens, but there are often numerous events that occur before anger erupts. Anger mapping is about recording the events that led up to an angry incident and what happened afterward, then identifying anger detours, or places where you could have made a different choice. By taking an anger detour, you are more likely to avoid negative consequences.

exercise: anger maps

Calm start: Start when your mood was okay and things were going well.

Pre-events: Write down all the significant events, both positive and negative, that happened throughout the day. Identify events that may have contributed to your rising anger or emotional risk.

Critical incident: Write down the main incident where you reacted to your anger.

Afterward: Write down what happened after the critical incident.

Detours: After you complete your anger map, go back and see where you could have taken anger detours. What might the alternative results have been?

This anger map is based on David's story from Activity 16. His calm start and pre-events have been added so you can see how they contribute to the critical incident. Under Anger Detours, we have listed several points at which David could have decided to respond in a more effective way.

	Events	Anger Detours
Calm Start	Went to bed the night before at 1:00 a.m.	Going to bed earlier so I can wake up on time
Pre-events	Woke up late for school	Setting my alarm
	Argued with Mom, forgot.my backpack	Putting my backpack near the door before going to bed
	Skipped school because I didn't have my homework	Going to school and explaining the problem to my teacher
	Hung out with friends and drank some beer	Staying at school, choosing not to drink
	Caught by Mom for skipping school and accused of drinking	Apologizing for my behavior
Critical Incident	Got into a huge fight with parents, punched a hole in the wall, missed concert	Leaving the argument before feeling out of control
Afterward	Grounded by parents, given in-school suspension	

David might consider the argument with his parents to be the cause of his problems. But if he had taken an anger detour at any point, the self-destructive behaviors leading up to the critical incident, and the incident itself, could have been avoided.

exercise: anger map

Use this blank anger map to map out what leads up to your angry behavior. Keep mapping your anger while you use this workbook. You can download additional copies at http://www.newharbinger.com/29163.

	Events	Anger Detours
Calm Start		
Pre-events		
Critical Incident		
Afterward		

exercise: zoom in, zoom out

After you have filled out a few anger maps, try this exercise.

Zoom In—Take a Closer Look

Pick an event from one of your anger maps. Zoom in, and try to identify what you were thinking, feeling, and experiencing in your body. Come up with alternative thoughts, feelings, and sensations.

People often have the same internal thought "distortions" that trigger their anger. Compare this anger map to other anger maps. Can you identify any patterns? Are there thoughts you repeatedly tell yourself, or feelings you repeatedly have?

Take some time to reflect on these themes and write down your thoughts in your journal.

Zoom Out—The Big Picture

If you have done several anger maps, take them out and compare them.

- Are there common situations in your anger maps?

- Do you notice common triggers in each of the maps?

- Are there situations that tend to cause you to have the greatest anger reaction?

- What consequences usually follow after the critical incidents?

If you like, you can write your observations down in your journal.

calming the body

Because anger is part of our primitive fight-or-flight survival instinct, our bodies act like a sort of alarm system, warning us when there is a threat. It is important to develop awareness skills so that you know you are becoming angry before your anger completely takes over. When you are self-aware, you can more effectively use body-focused techniques to calm down.

19 noticing anger in your body

Anger has a strong physical component and can show up in different ways for different people. When you get angry, you may experience some of these reactions. Check off the ones that you experience when you get angry.

- ☐ Tightness in muscles

- ☐ Dizziness

- ☐ Heavy, fast breathing

- ☐ Racing heart

- ☐ Sweating palms

- ☐ Grinding your teeth

- ☐ Crying

- ☐ Feeling your face getting hot

Being aware of the bodily sensations related to your anger can be one of the best tools to help keep your anger from getting out of control. The earlier you notice yourself starting to get angry, the better your chance of choosing to do something else.

informal practice: noticing your rising anger

During the next week, try to notice what you feel in your body when you become angry. Pay close attention to your anger at all levels. See if you can notice the subtle sensations you experience when you start to feel irritated. How do these sensations change as your anger increases? Are there different body sensations with different types of feelings? For example, does your face get flushed when you argue, but your stomach get tight when you feel threatened? Rate your level of anger on a scale of 1 to 5, 1 being the lowest and 5 the highest.

Date	Level of Anger	Sensations

20 your anger alarm

Anger serves as a natural alarm system. It may seem that anger erupts out of nowhere, like a volcano. But there are often early signs that anger is starting to build. These early signs can be thoughts, subtle feelings, or bodily sensations. We usually pay little attention to these. But when our anger has reached a dangerous level, it is often too late to control it. The better we become at noticing early signs, the better chance we have of making other choices to cool our anger.

This completed anger alarm chart can give you an idea of how thoughts, feelings, and bodily sensations rise up and intensify.

Level	Color	Thoughts	Feelings	Bodily Sensations
1	Blue	*I want to be left alone.* *Shut up.*	Annoyed	Tightness in chest Restlessness
2	Green	*I want to tell you off.* *Get away from me.*	Irritated	Jaw clenched Headache
3	Yellow	*Don't mess with me.* *I'm hurt and want to hurt someone else.*	Pissed off	Heart racing Face flushed Voice raised
4	Orange	*I can't believe you did that.* *I'm going to hurt someone.* *I hate you.*	Angry	Fist clenched Yelling Crying
5	Red	*I want to hit someone.* *I hate the world.*	Enraged	Heart pounding Shaking

exercise: identifying your anger alarms

Use the chart below to identify the different signals of your anger, from the earliest signs that you are getting upset to a full-blown explosive rage. You can use numbers from 1 to 5 to identify the different levels of your rising anger. Or you can visualize colors, like an alarm system going from blue to green to yellow to orange to red. Use whichever works to help you identify the different levels of your anger as it builds. Try to write down the thoughts, feelings, and bodily sensations that go with each level of your anger.

Level	Color	Thoughts	Feelings	Bodily Sensations
1	Blue			
2	Green			
3	Yellow			
4	Orange			
5	Red			

21 STOP

STOP (Stop, Take a breath, Observe what is happening in your body, Proceed) is a helpful tool that you can use anywhere. You can practice when you are bored or impatient. Or you can use this tool when you are annoyed and angry; for example, before you reply to an irritating text from your parent. When you use STOP, you can tolerate a greater range of feelings and relate to yourself and others with greater flexibility and openness.

informal practice: using STOP

At least a couple of times a day for a week, try practicing STOP at different times and in different situations, when things are calm, or when they get intense: Stop, Take a breath, Observe what is happening in your body, and Proceed.

Write your observations down in your journal. Were you more aware of your thoughts, feelings, and body sensations? If so, did this increased awareness affect how you reacted to situations?

breathing through anger 22

When we are in the middle of difficult emotions such as anger and fear, remembering to breathe through them can be challenging. But these few easy instructions can help: relax, observe, allow. Relax when you notice warning signs of anger in your body, such as tightness in the chest, a flushed face, or shallow breathing. Then observe: what is happening? Allow yourself to feel any emotions that may be beneath the surface of your anger. Each time you encounter an anger invitation, you can choose a different way to respond rather than react.

informal practice: relax, observe, allow

When you notice anger and other intense feelings rising, use this mindfulness exercise to breathe through the emotion.

- When you notice the warning signs of your anger, tell yourself to *relax*. Allow your body to relax. As you breathe in, count to four, and as you breathe out, count to six. Repeat: four in-breaths, six out-breaths. Feel your body relax and let go of tension.

- *Observe* what is happening while you relax. Stop thinking about why you are upset and simply allow the breath to rise and fall. Breathe in, breathe out. Ask yourself, *What is happening inside me right now?* Observe your bodily sensations.

- *Allow* yourself to feel the emotions that may be beneath your anger. Don't try to avoid them or cover them with anger. Just allow them to pass through you.

Try to envision your feelings as ice. Let the ice turn to water and the water to mist. With each breath, repeat: relax, observe, allow.

This mindfulness practice can prevent you from blowing up and causing more problems. It can also help you identify what is under the anger. All feelings are valid when you relax into what is happening within you and observe without reacting or avoiding. Feelings arise and pass away pretty quickly if we just allow them to pass through the mind and body. What was once an angry episode that would have caused much suffering for you and others can pass in minutes. This can help you to have more control over your feelings and more control over your life.

body scan 23

Our emotions are felt and experienced in our bodies. Intense emotions like anger and fear trigger body reactions that we may not even notice at times. Our bodies can also send us signals that inform us about how we are feeling even before our minds are aware of those feelings.

The goal of the body scan meditation is to simply become aware of the sensations in your body. Developing body awareness can be a powerful step toward accepting our feelings and reducing our impulsive reactions. You do not need to try to relax or change how you feel. You should not try to avoid difficult or unpleasant sensations. The goal is to become aware. Accept what you are feeling in different parts of your body. As you develop more awareness, you will notice how sensations come and go, how body sensations are always changing. Just like emotions, our physical sensations keep changing. If we let them be as they are, we are one step closer to deeper awareness and acceptance.

The body scan meditation has proven to be helpful for dealing with stress, physical pain, and sleep difficulties. This simple practice can be an important step in learning to cope with difficult emotions like anger, sadness, or anxiety.

formal practice: body scan meditation

The written instructions below are a simplified version of the full guided meditation that can be downloaded at http://www.newharbinger.com/29163. We recommend that you listen to the audio recording to get the full benefits of this meditation.

During this meditation, you will focus on the sensations of the body within the body. Start with the breath as an anchor. Scan through the body, exploring sensations as they arise. Body scanning is like a mental X-ray. By bringing awareness to each part of the body, you can tune in to layers of sensation.

Get started with these basic steps. Pause for about five breaths between each step.

- Get into a comfortable position (sitting or lying down). Shut your eyes if you like.

- Focus awareness on the breath. Breathe in … breathe out. Notice the rise and fall of your belly like a balloon inflating and deflating.

- Feet
  Bring awareness to whatever is felt in your feet: coolness, warmth, tingling, dryness. Notice whatever sensation is felt in this part of your body.

- Legs
  Scan up your legs: ankles, calves, thighs, and up to your hips. Bring awareness to what is felt.

- Hips, abdomen, torso
  Feel into your skin, muscles, and the organs beneath.

- Lower, then upper back
  Scan one vertebra at a time. Notice your ribs expand with each breath. Notice your heartbeat.

- Shoulders

  Gradually move down your arms, wrists, and hands. Extend awareness down to the tips of your fingers, then back up to your neck.

- Face

  In rings of awareness, move up your head, sensing into your jaw, your cheeks, your skull. Move through your chin, jaw, mouth, nose, cheeks, ears, and eyes. Notice what you feel in these places.

- Head

  Move from your forehead to the crown of your head, then down to the back of your head and neck.

- Whole body

  Expand awareness to your entire body, from toes to fingertips to top of the head. Breathe in, breathe out, feeling your entire body.

Body Scan Tips

- You may feel uncomfortable or unpleasant sensations, like itchiness or pain. Without avoiding or judging, allow these sensations to be.

- Notice how sensations pass and change when you allow them to be.

- If you get distracted, notice it, and then gently bring attention back to the body.

- Use the breath as an anchor when your attention wanders. Breathe in, and then come back to the body scan.

24 distraction

When your anger is building, and you feel unable to direct your awareness to what you are feeling without acting impulsively, distraction can help. The goal of distraction is to take your mind and heart away from what is upsetting you, and it can be a healthy coping strategy. Next time you feel your anger rising, try the following strategies to calm your body and reach emotional balance.

Distraction can take different forms, and you may find that particular forms work best for you or for certain types of situations. It is important to use the strategies that work, and also to keep them fresh by trying new distractions at times. Remember to use these strategies to distract yourself, not to try to fix the problem.

Here's a brief explanation of some different types of distraction:

Type of Distraction	What It Involves	Ideas
Change of Feelings	Activities that improve your mood	Listen to upbeat music. Watch an uplifting movie or TV show. Look at pictures of happy times in your life.
Mental Distraction	Activities that keep your thoughts occupied	Play a game on your smartphone. Read a good book. Learn about something online.
Physical Activities	Activities that help you expend energy in positive ways	Jog or go for a walk. Dance. Do yoga.
Connection	Activities that involve spending time with others (but not ruminating over whatever is upsetting you)	Call someone. Write an e-mail or letter. Meet a friend for lunch.
Humor	Activities that lower the emotional intensity of a situation and help you focus on the lighter side of life	Watch a funny video. Read online humor content.
Creativity	Activities that help you express yourself	Write a story or poem. Draw or paint. Work with clay.

skill practice: distraction strategies

In your journal, create a list of effective distraction strategies for you. How were you feeling before engaging in the distraction? How did you feel afterward? Were you better able to respond rather than react to the upsetting situation?

grounding 25

Intense feelings like anger and fear can cause you to feel out of control. You may lose the ability to think clearly, or you may have a flushed face, a racing heart, and rapid breathing. When you feel overwhelmed by intense feelings, you can use these strategies to help ground yourself in your body and your immediate surroundings. Try to do these activities mindfully, which means staying in the present moment and remaining nonjudgmental.

Grounding Strategies	
Hold a piece of ice.	Count backward from twenty.
Take a hot shower.	Snap a rubber band on your wrist.
Name objects in the room.	Eat mindfully.
Count your breaths in and out.	Walk mindfully.
Watch clouds.	Touch your toes.
Splash cold water on your face.	Use the STOP tool.
Name what you are doing.	Notice your body sensations.

skill practice: grounding strategies

Try different grounding strategies and write down how effective each one was in your journal. Use the questions below to guide your reflections.

- How were you feeling before the grounding activity? What were your sensations and thoughts?

- How did you feel afterward?

- How were you able to move forward to handle what was in front of you?

Your body may be very stressed from handling so much anger. Finding ways to soothe yourself can ease the tension and allow you to feel more calm and relaxed. Try to engage your different senses when using self-soothing strategies. Treat yourself to some of these strategies, and create a list of your favorites.

Self-Soothing Strategies	
Play calming music.	Consciously relax your body, one part at a time.
Take a hot bath or shower.	Go out in nature.
Light incense or heat scented oils.	Pick fresh flowers.
Cook a tasty meal.	Take a nap.
Slowly eat something you really like.	Look at artwork.
Relax with a movie or book.	Get a massage.

skill practice: self-soothing

During the next week, try to do at least one self-soothing activity a day. See if you find that you're better able to handle challenges and frustrations after making the time to take care of yourself. Try different strategies and, using these questions, write in your journal about how effective each one was.

- How does your body feel after doing self-soothing activities?

- How do self-soothing activities help you handle your anger and other intense emotions?

- How do self-soothing activities improve your attitude?

releasing 27

Anger and other intense feelings build up in the body and are often expressed physically, perhaps as tight muscles, hitting, or screaming. Finding healthy ways to release this built-up tension can be very useful in managing anger. Releasing strategies are activities that can help you channel the physical energy created by anger.

Releasing Strategies	
Sports	Yoga
Skateboarding	Tai chi
Snowboarding	Martial arts
Running	Hiking
Dancing	Massage
Walking	Biking
Aerobics	Swimming
Cleaning	Building, fixing, or repairing something

skill practice: releasing strategies

When you feel tension building, try to do one of these physical releasing activities, or others that you like to do. See if you can schedule a regular time to do some of these. Try different strategies and, in your journal, write about how effective each one was. These questions can guide your responses.

- How do regular physical activities affect your bodily reactions to anger?

- What releasing activities can you do regularly?

- What can you do when you feel your anger rising?

- How do you feel after engaging in these releasing activities?

clearing the mind

How we think about a situation affects how we feel, and then how we react. Sometimes our thoughts are correct views of what is happening around us. At other times, our minds can distort what we see. It is important to pay close attention to your thoughts. Then you can sift through them and decide which is the most clear and helpful.

28 cooling wisdom

When we are full of anger, our thoughts are distorted by how we feel. Thought provokers are negative thought patterns, habits of the mind that tend to fuel our anger. They can cause you to expect the worst from others and from situations. It is important that you train yourself to view things more clearly without angry distortions. The cooling-wisdom skills below can be an antidote to thoughts that provoke you.

Thought Provokers	Cooling Wisdom
Labels and judgments: These short statements (like "My dad's a jerk!") prevent us from accurately describing situations or the actions of others.	Describe: Be descriptive rather than judgmental. Observing and describing what has happened rather than using labels allows you to see more options and perspectives.
Absolutes: These statements, which use words like "never" and "always," make everything black or white and leave no room for negotiation. Absolutes build opposition and conflict.	Look for exceptions: Try to find exceptions to this black-or-white thinking. Exceptions give you hope for possibilities and choices.
Mind reading: This is convincing yourself that you know what others are thinking and feeling and why they act the way they do, without actual evidence.	Ask, don't assume: Before you assume what someone else's intentions are and get upset, try to ask directly what that person's motivation is. As the saying goes, when you A-S-S-U-M-E, you make an ASS out of U and ME.
Catastrophizing: This means blowing things out of proportion and imagining that the worst possible outcome will take place. This style of thinking amplifies anxiety and anger.	Be optimistic: Focus on the likelihood of things going well rather than predicting the worst. Balance worry with the real evidence of times when things worked out.

Keith's Story: Self-Judgment

Keith gets a D on his English midterm even though he studied. When he gets home, his parents are congratulating his older sister, who got into a really good college. Keith thinks to himself, I'm an idiot and a loser. *He leaves the house to get high with his friends.*

Keith's Story Rewritten:
The Cooling Wisdom of Description

After Keith gets a D, he goes to see his teacher because he studied hard for this test. His teacher tells him that most of the class got below a C, and he will be adjusting the grades. Keith leaves thinking, That was a hard test, *instead of* I'm an idiot.

exercise: what are your thought provokers?

Tell about a conflict or an upsetting situation you got into in the past week.

_____

_____

_____

Which thought provoker might you have used that made the situation worse?

_____

_____

_____

What might have happened if you used a cooling-wisdom strategy instead?

_____

_____

_____

informal practice: removing the judgment

During the next week, be aware of your judgments. Notice the ways you judge people and situations. Remind yourself when you are making a judgment. Practice turning your judgments into more balanced descriptions.

turning hot thoughts into cool ones 29

Anger is like a fire whose flames are fed or starved by thoughts. The words inside our heads can cause our flames of anger to rage, or they can stamp out the fire. When we get angry, the first thoughts we have are usually hot thoughts and they are automatic. We get mad, then we start talking to ourselves about being mad; for example, by thinking, *That's not fair!*, *I hate that!*, or *I never get what I want!* Hot thoughts feed anger, making it grow.

On the other hand, cool thoughts are like sprinkling water on the flames. Cool thoughts are messages you say inside your head to feel better and calm down; for example, *I can deal with this*, *this isn't worth getting mad about*, or *I'll survive.*

exercise: turning hot thoughts into cool thoughts

Here's an example: Your mother makes you clean the garage before you can hang out with your friends.

Hot thought: *I hate her! My friends will be gone by the time I'm done. This sucks!*

Cool thought: *Most of the mess is mine, so it's fair that I clean it up. I can see my friends another time.*

For each situation, come up with a hot thought you might have, then replace it with a cool thought.

You forget your homework and your teacher gives you an F instead of letting you hand it in late.

Your hot thought: _____

Your cool thought: _____

You find out that your best friend went to the mall with another classmate and never told you.

Your hot thought: _____

Your cool thought: _____

You get a text from your friend, saying *Thx a lot for remembering to meet me after school! U only think about urself!*

Your hot thought: _____

Your cool thought: _____

skill practice: hot to cool thoughts

During the next week, notice the hot thoughts that come into your mind and feed your anger. Practice coming up with cool thoughts in these situations.

Write down your most common hot thoughts and the most effective cool thoughts below.

My Most Common Hot Thoughts	My Most Effective Cool Thoughts

30 RAIN

Another way to find what motivates anger and begin to address it is known as RAIN (Recognize, Allow, Investigate, and Nonpersonalize). Each of these components can help you see what happens when you get angry, without becoming lost in the emotional content of the story behind your anger—like watching a movie about what is happening rather than being in the movie. Sometimes your anger will get away from you, and you can practice after the fact to be better prepared for next time. For example, if you have already blown up and perhaps regret your words or actions, you can begin to recognize right then.

A basic principle of mindfulness is that we cannot experience freedom from anger unless we recognize that it is happening. Whenever you notice signs of your anger building, practice RAIN:

- Recognize when you are beginning to experience intense feelings and impulses in the body. These are your body's warning signs. When you recognize, you are asking, *What is happening right now (inside of me)?* The more you learn to recognize the range of emotions, the more comfortable you become with them. You stop being hijacked by intense feelings.

- Allow your anger to be without reacting to it. Just try to ride out the wave of anger without doing anything about it yet.

- Investigate the body sensations, thoughts, or feelings associated with your anger. Notice where in the body you feel anger. (You can use the Body Scan Meditation from Activity 23.) Notice the thoughts that come into your mind. What images come up and what do you tell yourself? Notice the emotions that rise up, without getting swept up by them.

- Nonpersonalize your anger by reminding yourself, *I am not this anger, and this anger is not me.* This anger just is; don't take it personally. Like all other emotions, it comes and goes, like waves on the ocean. Let go of owning your anger, and don't let it possess you.

Here's an example of how RAIN could be used in a common conflict:

Your father keeps telling you to do your homework, but you are busy and say you will do it later. Your mother reminds you soon after, raising her voice. As you start to get angry, you choose to practice RAIN: Recognize—*I'm getting frustrated*; Allow—*I feel like I'm being nagged*; Investigate—*My shoulders feel tight*; Nonpersonalize—*My parents aren't saying I'm bad or wrong. Maybe they're frustrated because I'm ignoring them.*

Then you can choose to respond rather than react. You might explain that you are busy but will do what they ask in fifteen minutes (and do it).

When we can use RAIN effectively, we can begin to see what is happening in every moment without a layer of reaction or judgment. Life does not always go our way. We have to come into some acceptance of this. RAIN can help us better navigate difficult emotions and situations.

exercise: applying RAIN
to a common conflict

Describe a common conflict you have been part of.

_____

_____

Then tell how you could apply RAIN in this conflict.

Recognize: _____

_____

Allow: _____

_____

Investigate: _____

_____

Nonpersonalize: _____

_____

mindfulness of thoughts 31

Our thoughts are often on automatic pilot, and we can fall into habits of thinking and perceiving. This mindfulness practice will help you simply notice the nature of your thoughts and develop increased awareness of your thought processes. Use this practice to observe thoughts without clinging to them or pushing them away. Just acknowledge them and let them be without judgment.

formal practice: mindfulness of thoughts

The written instructions below are a simplified version of the full guided meditation that can be downloaded at http://www.newharbinger.com/29163. We recommend that you listen to the audio recording to get the full benefits of this meditation.

Get started with these basic steps. Pause for about five breaths between each step.

- Get into a comfortable position (sitting or lying down). Shut your eyes if you like.

- Focus awareness on the breath. Breathe in; breathe out. Connect with the breath at either the tip of the nose or the rise and fall of the belly. When attention strays off the breath, gently bring it back to the focus of meditation.

- Be aware of the sensation. Is it pleasant, unpleasant, or neutral? Bring awareness to feeling tones in your mind and body.

- Contemplate the moment-to-moment experience as pleasant, unpleasant, or neutral. Notice the changing nature of feelings as well as thoughts and sensations.

32 big sky meditation

This guided meditation practice can help you allow your thoughts to be without anxiously clinging to them or angrily pushing them away. A key principle of mindfulness is that everything changes. The thoughts or feelings we experience in one moment that feel unbearable will change in the next moment. Just like sensations in our bodies change, the sounds around us come and go. The Big Sky Meditation can help us expand our awareness to allow the space for all that we think, feel, and experience.

formal practice: big sky meditation

The written instructions below are a simplified version of the full guided meditation that can be downloaded at http://www.newharbinger.com/29163. We recommend that you listen to the audio recording to get the full benefits of this meditation. Get started with these basic steps. Pause for about five breaths between each step.

- Get into a comfortable position (sitting or lying down). Shut your eyes if you like. Focus awareness on the breath. Breathe in ... breathe out. As thoughts arise, notice the thoughts and return to the breath.

- Notice the comings and goings of sounds.

- Imagine the mind as a big blue sky. Imagine thoughts, sounds, or bodily sensations as clouds moving through the sky of the mind.

- Imagine the breath as a gentle breeze moving clouds through the sky of the mind.

- Let thoughts, feelings, and memories just drift through the big sky like clouds.

noting 33

The intention of this practice is to sit quietly and observe whatever arises naturally. You don't have to think about anything or force yourself to experience anything. The purpose of this mindfulness activity is to develop your skills of awareness of all of the big and small experiences you have as they emerge.

informal practice: noting meditation

Get started with these basic steps. Spend a few minutes on each step.

- Get into a comfortable position (sitting or lying down). Shut your eyes if you like. Focus awareness on the breath. Breathe in; breathe out.

- Note sensations as they rise and fall away. Acknowledge them with a simple phrase like *tight jaw* or *aching back muscles*.

- Note thoughts and let them be. Do not try to grasp or push away the thoughts. Just note what you are thinking, with labels like *worrying* or *thinking*. Imagine thoughts like leaves drifting down a river, passing you by.

- Turn your attention to emotions, noting feelings and letting them be. Simply note things like *tired* or *peaceful* or *sad*. Note the feelings without analyzing why you are having them or pushing them away.

- Return to the breath again and again.

maintaining emotional balance

People with problems managing anger are usually very sensitive. You may be more sensitive than your friends, and more vulnerable to becoming overly emotional. In this chapter we will help you understand your emotions better and develop skills for regulating how you feel.

34 your emotional health

Certain lifestyle habits (for example, those that make us intoxicated, exhausted, or continually hungry) or social environments can make us more vulnerable to becoming upset. Others can keep us more emotionally healthy and protect us from emotional triggers.

exercise: emotional health or emotional risk?

Fill out this quiz to see if your lifestyle habits and social environment support emotional health or emotional risk.

1.	I get enough sleep most nights.	Yes	No
2.	I drink or use drugs more than two times a week, often when I feel upset.	Yes	No
3.	I exercise or do physical activity at least once a week.	Yes	No
4.	Things I used to like don't make me happy anymore.	Yes	No
5.	I have a close friend or adult I can talk to about my problems.	Yes	No
6.	I play video games or watch TV more than ten hours a week.	Yes	No
7.	I eat healthy and try not to over- or undereat.	Yes	No
8.	I live in a violent neighborhood or attend a dangerous school.	Yes	No
9.	I feel capable in school or at work.	Yes	No
10.	There is a lot of yelling or tension in my home.	Yes	No

Emotional Health Score: _____ (number of "Yes" answers for the odd-numbered questions)

Emotional Risk Score: _____ (number of "Yes" answers for the even-numbered questions)

If your emotional risk score is higher than your emotional health score, try engaging in more of the positive activities listed here, and reducing the habits that can put you more at risk.

- Fun—Movies, concerts, BBQs, parties
  Activities that get you to laugh and have fun will improve your mood and emotional health.

- Creative expression—Writing, drawing, dance, or playing music
  These activities can help you express your emotions in healthier and more artistic ways than angry outbursts. Creative expression is one of the most effective ways to understand your emotions.

- Physical activities—Exercise, sports, hiking, walking
  Physical exercise has been proven to improve mood and reduce stress.

- Spending time with friends—Going to a movie or concert, meeting for coffee

  Spending time with friends, especially doing something together, improves emotional health.

People who tend to get angry easily also tend to be unhappy a lot of the time. The world may seem like an unpleasant place. You may spend more of your time hating your life than loving it. That is why it is so important to make yourself do things that make you feel good and allow you to express yourself. You may not always have the energy or motivation to do these positive activities, but studies show that if you do them, your mood will most often improve afterward.

exercise: positive activities plan

For the next week, identify a positive activity you will do for each day of the week. Rate your mood from 1 (lowest) to 5 (happiest) before and after doing the activity.

	Positive Activity	Mood (Before and After)
Monday		
Tuesday		
Wednesday		
Thursday		
Friday		
Saturday		
Sunday		

accepting yourself and all your feelings 35

Why do I get so upset? How often do you secretly ask yourself this question? After you blame other people and situations, we bet this question remains. You may wonder, *Why don't my friends get as upset as I do?* or *What's wrong with me?* The good news is you are not alone. There are some real reasons why your emotions may feel so out of control sometimes. There may be a mismatch between your wiring (biology) and the way people respond to you (environment). Think of it as two mismatched pieces in a puzzle.

Your wiring may have meant that, growing up, you were more sensitive to certain experiences and easily upset by changes. Maybe you were highly active with a lot of energy. Or maybe you were the opposite: more cautious and quiet. Your childhood tendencies are part of your temperament and affect how you relate to others.

Caregivers and other adults may not have known how to respond to your sensitivity. Your parents may have been unable to soothe you when you were upset or to handle your energy level. Or maybe you had a parent who was not there for you because of illness. Even when adults try to cheer children up, they often don't allow them to truly share their sad feelings. Mismatches like these may have created a situation where your needs and feelings were not responded to with understanding. You got the message that what you feel and express is not okay.

When people around us invalidate our experiences or do not accept our feelings, we may turn those messages against ourselves. We fail to learn how to identify and accept what we are feeling inside. We don't get practice managing those unacceptable feelings. The result is feeling emotionally out of control.

If You...	You May Tell Yourself...
Are very sensitive or easily upset	*There's something wrong with me.*
Often experience intense anger or impulsivity	*I hate everyone.*
Have difficulty calming down	*I can't handle anything. I'm a mess.*
Have difficulty managing feelings	*I don't fit in. No one understands me.*

exercise: identifying negative messages you received

In each family, there are certain feelings that are not acceptable to express or experiences that are not tolerated. Sometimes the disapproval is outright; other times the communication is nonverbal. Look at the list below and check the feelings or experiences that were unacceptable in your family.

☐ Sadness	☐ Humor or silliness	☐ Loneliness
☐ Anger or disagreement	☐ Frustration	☐ Need for space
☐ Independence	☐ Not understanding	☐ Physical weakness
☐ Need for closeness	☐ Success	
☐ Failure or mistakes	☐ Pride	

Take a moment to write down some of the messages you received, whether directly or indirectly, about the feelings or experiences you marked as unacceptable.

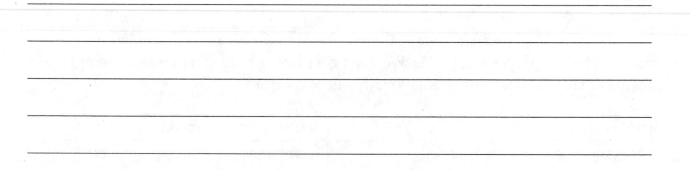

informal practice: accepting your feelings now

The first step toward managing your feelings is to truly accept them. From the mindfulness perspective, this is where the two basic questions come in: What am I feeling right now, inside of me? Can I stick with it?

- Find a quiet place where you can spend from five to fifteen minutes reflecting. Select one of your feelings and try to get in touch with it.

- Tell yourself, *It's all right for me to* … (complete the sentence with your own meaningful feeling or experience). Accept the message in your body and your heart.

- Investigate and identify any negative messages you tell yourself about having this feeling.

- Allow yourself to deeply feel your own acceptance of this feeling or experience. Repeat: *It's all right for me to…*

As you go through your week, practice RAIN—Recognize, Allow, Investigate, Nonpersonalize—to manage these feelings.

36 softening the heart

When you are driven by your emotions, your thoughts are distorted by how you feel. You can get into painful habits of the heart—ways of reacting to situations that tend to make you more upset. We call these emotional upsetters. Blame is one of the most common upsetters because it is a way to avoid what we are really feeling, and our part in causing it. We can avoid responsiblity by blaming everything wrong on someone else; or we can beat ourselves up with self-blame, not holding others accountable for their part in the conflict. Your heart can be hardened by the chronic bitterness of anger and resentment. These softening-the-heart strategies can be an antidote to negative feelings.

Emotional Upsetter	Softening-the-Heart Strategies
Focusing on the past or future: Getting angry about something small because of past resentments you may hold on to, or future fears of what might happen, prevent you from just dealing with what is going on right now.	Focusing on the present: Focus attention on the immediate situation rather than clouding what is happening with past pains or future worries.
Discounting the positive, exaggerating the negative: These two go hand in hand. An example is when you say something positive, then use the word "but" followed by a negative statement; for example, "I got a good grade on my last math test, but I didn't deserve it. I was just lucky."	Thinking positively: Try to find the good and look for possibilities in a situation rather than what is wrong or threatening. Follow this wise suggestion: try to see the glass as half full, not half empty.
Following the "shoulds": This upsetter involves having a list of unbreakable rules for yourself or others to live by. Flexibility in your expectations of your own and others' behaviors will lead to many fewer anger invitations.	Being flexible: Be willing to hear other views rather than rigidly holding to your personal rules of behavior.

exercise: looking at your emotional upsetters

Describe a recent situation where you used an emotional upsetter.

_____

_____

_____

_____

_____

What effect did that have on the situation?

_____

_____

_____

_____

What might have happened if you had used a heart-softening strategy instead?

_____

_____

_____

_____

skill practice: focusing on the good

During the next week, try to notice your tendency to be negative. Is your first thought *What could go wrong*? Is your first reaction to others *What bad thing could they do to me*?

Try to shift this tendency by focusing on what could go right. What is the opportunity instead of the danger? Start off thinking that others have good intentions. See if this helps you feel better and avoid conflict.

acting against your angry urges 37

How often have you realized a day after an angry outburst that your feelings were more intense than the situation required? A few hours later, or a day later, you may have said to yourself, *Why was I so mad?*

When we act on our initial intense feelings, we often do things we later regret. Intense emotions like anger can lead to urges to act aggressively (either toward others, property, or yourself). However, acting on these violent urges often makes the situation worse. Rather than taking actions that intensify the emotion, the best approach is to take an opposite action.

Tyler's Story: Reacting in a Way That Helps

Tyler and his girlfriend, Julia, get into an argument like many of their other ones. Julia is angry with Tyler because he hung out with his friends so long that he was late to meet up with her. When these arguments start, Tyler usually gets extremely defensive, yells at Julia, and brings up all the times she has canceled on him. This time, Tyler acts against his angry urge; he goes for a walk to distract himself. When he returns, he apologizes and promises to call next time he is running late. Julia agrees not to get on his case if he calls first. What usually turns into a huge fight remains small and manageable.

exercise: acting against angry urges

During the next week, write down conflicts that come up. You can use your CALM log for events (see Activity 17). Describe your angry urge, and rate its intensity from 1 (lowest) to 5 (highest). Tell whether you acted on the urge, and what the outcome was. Finally, write down an opposite action you could have taken.

Conflict	Angry Urge	Intensity (1–5)	Acted On? (Yes or No)	Outcome	Opposite Action

mindfulness of emotions 38

Intense emotions can often overcome us so that we end up reacting before we are fully aware of what we are feeling. Developing mindfulness of emotions can provide some of the deepest insight into our inner selves. This mindfulness practice can increase your awareness of what you are truly feeling and lead to more emotional peace, freedom, and choice in how you respond to others.

formal practice: mindfulness of emotions

The written instructions below are a simplified version of the full guided meditation that can be downloaded at http://www.newharbinger.com/29163. We recommend that you listen to the audio recording to get the full benefits of this meditation.

Get started with these basic steps. Pause for a few minutes between each step.

- Take a posture that will bring both relaxation and alertness.

- Direct your attention to the breath. Connect with the breath at the tip of the nose or the rise and fall of the belly. Breathe in … breathe out.

- Explore the feeling of each thought, sensation, and emotion.

- Explore deeper into your feelings. Recognize what feeling is present as it arises. Allow the emotion for what it is. Investigate where the emotion is felt in the body and thought in the mind. Nonpersonalize and step back from the emotion as not part of your self. (See Activity 30 for more guidance.)

- Notice how emotions change from moment to moment. Watch your feelings change like the weather. Consider how thoughts and emotions are not permanent, but always changing.

39 your emotional fire extinguisher

When you are in a conflict, it can be hard to use the coping skills you have been learning. But if you plan ahead, you can prepare yourself for the situation and be ready to do something different. You can use your emotional fire extinguisher to put out a conflict before it starts.

Xavier's Story: Reacting to Mom's Freak-out

Almost every week Xavier gets into an argument with his mom about going out with his friends on the weekend. At first she tells him he can go, but when the time comes, she asks him a lot of questions, like "Where are you going?" or "Will parents be there?" Xavier gets irritated by the questions, and his mom gets more anxious that something bad will happen or that he will be with the "wrong" people. These arguments usually end with Xavier slamming doors, and his mother saying that he can't go out because of his behavior and that she can't trust him.

Xavier's Story Rewritten: Putting Out the Fire Before It Starts

Knowing that his mom is going to ask a lot of questions, Xavier decides to plan ahead and use his emotional fire extinguisher. He reminds himself that she asks him so many questions because she is concerned, not because she is mean. This reminder is an emotional fire extinguisher that keeps him from feeling defensive and reactive. Three days in advance, Xavier tells his mom what the plan is and which friends he will be with. He says that he knows she worries about him and he promises to check in by text when he gets there, and if they go anywhere else. He tries to validate her worry and explain that he will be responsible. Since his mom feels understood, she is a little less intense, and there is no big fight between them. She lets Xavier go out as planned.

exercise: future conflict or challenging situation

Each of us has situations that we can predict will upset us; there are patterns to our anger. Look over your CALM log or anger maps to identify your own examples.

Write down a difficult event or situation that you anticipate will happen during the next week.

_____

_____

_____

Explain what typically happens during these situations. Who is involved? What is the usual outcome?

_____

_____

_____

Explain how you would like to see the situation happen instead.

_____

_____

_____

Describe your emotional fire extinguisher—the specific skill or strategy you could use to put out the fire of your anger in this situation.

_____

_____

_____

40 pain is inevitable, suffering optional

Our society teaches us that we should do everything we can to avoid any kind of pain. Feel bad? Buy new clothes or the latest gadget. Upset? Take something to help you feel better. The reality is that painful experiences, such as disappointment, loss, or crisis, are part of life, and our attempts to avoid pain often cause us more suffering.

These simple formulas depict the point:

Pain + Avoidance = Suffering

Pain + Acceptance = Healing and Growth

Anger often covers up another feeling we want to avoid. When this happens, anger is a secondary emotion; it comes after the underlying primary emotion and can be so strong that we may not even know the primary emotion is there. The problem is that anger won't fix the feeling beneath the surface. That's why we might get enraged about something and explode, but still feel no better afterward.

Tracy's Story: Avoidance

Tracy's boyfriend, Joshua, recently broke up with her. Tracy doesn't want to feel the pain of losing the relationship, so she has been partying with her friends every day and dating other guys. At home, she is getting into more and more fights with her family. Whenever her friends or family ask how she is doing after the breakup, she says, "It doesn't matter; I didn't really like him anyway. I don't want to talk about it."

Tracy's Story Rewritten: Acceptance

Tracy recognizes that she is very sad and angry after Joshua breaks up with her. She spends some time writing in her journal about how she feels. Tracy also spends time with her best friend, talking about how difficult the breakup has been. She wants to quit the school volleyball team and avoid everyone. But instead she sticks to her commitment and, after each practice, she feels a little better. Over time, Tracy begins to heal.

exercise: the feelings beneath the surface

Read the following situations that involve primary and secondary feelings. The first one has been completed as an example. For the others, see if you can guess what each person's primary emotion is: (a) embarrassment, (b) sadness, or (c) disappointment. After the secondary angry response, try to think of a different way the person could respond that is more closely related to the primary emotion.

Another student accidentally trips Mary in the school hallway. The first emotion Mary feels is *embarrassment*, but she instantly screams at the girl who tripped her, threatening to beat her up.

If Mary focused on her primary emotion, she could have *smiled and said, "That was embarrassing!"*

Sarah was really looking forward to meeting up with her friends at the teen center on Friday night, but her mom says that she doesn't trust her out that late. The first emotion Sarah feels is _____. She has a total meltdown and calls her mom names. She gets grounded for the entire weekend.

If Sarah focused on her primary emotion, she might have _____

_____

Hunter's mom was very sick with cancer during his junior year of high school. His first feeling was _____ because he thought he might lose his mom. He stayed angry and irritable so that no one would try to talk with him about it. At times he would just destroy things in his room or steal.

If Hunter focused on his primary emotion, he might have _____

_____

informal practice: acknowledging your pain without causing more suffering

Think through the questions below and write your reflections in your journal.

Think of a time you got angry in the past week. What was your primary emotion?

How did you try to avoid this painful experience?

Did you cause yourself more suffering?

What could have happened if you had simply acknowledged the initial pain?

turning toward your anger and away from blame 41

How often have you said, "He made me angry" or "I wouldn't have gotten so mad if …"? We often blame our anger on other people or circumstances. We look outward for its cause, not inward. We also tend to look outward for someone or something to make us feel better, to fix the angry, unpleasant, frustrated feelings we have inside.

The problem is that we cannot control others or change every situation. But if we practice turning our attention inward toward our anger, we can learn a great deal from it. And we can learn to change how we feel because we won't depend so much on what others do or if things go the way we want.

Erica's Story: It's Not My Fault

Erica got caught with weed in her locker at school. She was suspended and her parents were contacted. They have grounded her from going on a trip with her friends. She is furious, insisting that the school had no right going through her stuff. She tells her parents it was no big deal, and that it is their fault she even smoked because they make her miserable. She blames everyone for what happened—except herself.

Erica's Story Rewritten: Turning Toward Anger

After Erica gets caught with weed and sent home, she sits in her bedroom. At first she is furious at the principal, her parents, everyone. Then she writes in her journal about her anger and realizes that under her anger she feels ashamed. She feels stupid for what she did and for letting down her parents and teachers. The next day she apologizes to her parents. She explains how down she has been feeling lately. Even though she still can't go on the trip with her friends, she feels better after talking to her parents.

informal practice: turning toward anger

The next time you find yourself getting angry, try to bring your attention inward to the actual feeling you are experiencing rather than outward to the person you think is "causing" it. Use mindfulness practices like STOP or RAIN to acknowledge what is happening without getting swept up in the emotion or drama. Sit in a quiet space and take a moment to fill in these statements. Pause for a few minutes between each statement, and let your response rise to awareness.

- Without blaming anyone else, I am angry because I feel...

- Deep down, I really feel...

- Deep, deep down, I feel...

- I can take care of myself by...

kind connections

When we believe we are angry, we will continue to act angry. But if we can learn to shift our attention to love and kindness toward ourselves and others, we'll find that we don't get angry as often and have less conflict with others.

Mindfulness can lessen our attachment to anger, allowing us to be more open to the good in ourselves and in others (even those who piss us off). By increasing our ability to be kind and patient, we will be more kind and patient with ourselves. As we develop more compassion for ourselves, we will naturally have more available for others who struggle. So it's a win-win.

In this chapter we will look at ways to stop separating ourselves from others and using fear and anger as a protection against being hurt.

42 seeking connection

A fight has two sides. Conflict is caused by a "me against you" way of looking at things. Often, a simple disagreement builds into an all-out fight because the more we feel someone is against us, the stronger we fight back. These conflict instigators are a few of the ways we make situations worse. The connection-seeking strategies are healthier ways to resolve conflict.

Conflict Instigators	Connection-Seeking Strategies
Blaming: Blaming involves holding others responsible for your pain or holding yourself responsible for the problems of others. Remember, the only person you can control is you. Blaming fuels conflict by accusing someone else of being responsible for your feelings.	Personal responsibility: Focus on your reactions and your part in a conflict. They are really the only things you can change. Strive to reach peaceful solutions.
Taking sides: This black-and-white thinking leads to viewing every interaction as a battle, with people either on your side or against you. It prevents healthy negotiations.	"Both-and" instead of "either-or" thinking: Move away from "either-or" thinking to "both-and" thinking. Try substituting the word "but" with the word "and."
Defensiveness: When you are defensive, you feel like the finger of blame is directed at you. Defensiveness involves taking every statement as a personal attack rather than listening and responding.	Nonpersonalizing: Try not to take every statement or situation personally, or as a criticism. Step back and try to see the grain of truth without being defensive.

Max's Story: No One Is on My Side!

Max has been grounded for getting a D in science. When his dad refuses to let him go out with his girlfriend, Max asks his mom, who also refuses. Max shouts, "No one is ever on my side!" He glares at his mom and refuses to say another word.

Max's Story Rewritten: Taking Both Sides

Max says to his parents, "I know my grade needs to improve and I would really like to spend time with my girlfriend. If I show you I've done all my homework for the week, can I go out on Friday?"

Certain words divide us, other words bring us together. When we use the word "but," we usually cancel out whatever positive thing we may have communicated; for example, "I know you get nervous and would really like me home by curfew, *but* I want to stay at the party because everyone will still be there." This statement sets up a conflict between the two perspectives and is likely to make the other person more upset. Any attempt at understanding is wiped away because of that "but." However, when we use the word "and," we share our own perspective and we communicate that we understand the other person's; for example, "I would like to stay at the party because everyone will still be there, *and* I know you get nervous and would really like me home by curfew." This statement allows for negotiation and compromise.

skill practice: substituting "and" for "but"

During the next week, try this very simple and powerful technique. Every time you would normally use the word "but," try substituting "and." You will likely be amazed by how effectively it prevents conflicts from getting bigger.

For example:

- Show that you understand what someone is feeling *and* that you have feelings also. ("Dad, I know you're upset because I failed my test, *and* I feel like I tried my best and it was a really hard test.")

- Explain that you see another person's view of a situation *and* how you see it. ("I know that you feel I haven't been around much *and* I feel that I've tried to reach you even though I've been really busy.")

- Acknowledge someone else's suggestion *and* share your own. ("I hear that you would really like to go to the mall *and* I was really looking forward to seeing the movie that just came out.")

deepening the well of understanding 43

Anger causes us to have a shallow well of understanding. We have less tolerance for others and, more important, for our own difficulties. When we take sides, it's really hard to see the other person's viewpoint. Although being understanding may feel like giving up, the truth is that empathy and compassion can be more effective in resolving conflict than acting strong or threatening. Empathy is showing others that you get what they are experiencing and feeling. Compassion further communicates that you care for their suffering. This level of understanding will put out the flames of your own anger and reduce the tension between you and others.

formal practice: may you be happy

For the next week, when you are confronted with an anger invitation, try the following before reacting:

- Take a deep breath in, counting to four. Then breathe out, counting to six.

- Recognize that the person who is annoying you may be suffering. Maybe he had a bad day or she got some hard news.

- Try to wish the person well. You can say silently or out loud, "May you be happy" or "I'm sorry you are hurting."

This practice can have a profound effect on you and others. Try it out and see how you change.

formal practice: walking in another's shoes

During the next week, if you find yourself holding a grudge or feeling resentful of someone, try this compassion practice:

- Find a quiet place where you can be alone for a few minutes.

- Think of the person you are having a conflict with and the difficult situation you are struggling with.

- Acknowledge how you are feeling about the conflict, but do not hold on to this feeling for too long. Use your wise mind to create some space so you do not get swept up by emotion. Imagine setting your feelings aside someplace safe for a moment.

- Now, try to imagine how the situation looks and feels from the other person's viewpoint. Why might this person have different needs and fears?

- Spend a few moments imagining what life is like for the other person. What is her life story? What would it be like to walk in his shoes for a day?

- End the practice wishing that both of you can be happy and free from suffering.

effective communication
44

The way you communicate with others has a lot to do with anger. Effective communication lets you express difficult feelings, allowing the flames of anger to die down and go out. Ineffective communication can be like throwing gasoline on a fire. It can cause your anger to grow and cause more conflict. Below are four different ways that people communicate and deal with conflict.

- Passive

  If you are a passive person, you often bottle up your emotions instead of expressing them. You may be afraid that you will upset someone by expressing how you really feel. Passive people want to get along at all costs and may sacrifice their own needs, values, or goals to keep others happy. After a conflict, they may be left feeling resentful or walked over.

- Aggressive

  If you are an aggressive person, you may express your emotions in a hostile or dominating way. Aggressive people may get their way, but it is at the expense of others. They can be intimidating and threatening, sometimes without even knowing it. Aggressive people insist on being "right," winning, or getting their way. After a conflict, they may feel guilty or ashamed.

- Passive-Aggressive

  If you tend to be passive-aggressive, you express your anger through more indirect ways. Passive-aggressive people avoid expressing how they feel directly, usually because they fear rejection or conflict. They may get the message across that they are mad without actually saying the words; for example, by giving someone the silent treatment or storming off.

- Assertive

  When you're assertive, you express your thoughts, feelings, and opinions in a clear, direct, honest way. If you are being assertive, you tend to be respectful toward both the other person and yourself. Assertive people are confident, yet are good listeners and willing to negotiate.

exercise: what's your communication style?

These questions can help you figure out what your communication style is. Put check marks next to the ones that seem to describe you best. When you're finished, add up the number of check marks for each section to see which style you use most often.

Passive

☐ I worry that if I express how I really feel, I will upset people or lose relationships.

☐ I often feel like it is not worth the effort to express disagreement or hurt feelings.

☐ I worry more about keeping everyone else happy than myself.

☐ Other people often make decisions for me.

☐ I bottle up my feelings instead of expressing them to others, especially disagreement.

Total: _____

Aggressive

☐ Friends and family are often afraid of upsetting me.

☐ My first priority is getting what I want, regardless of how it affects others.

☐ I often yell, swear, threaten, or use other aggressive ways to communicate.

☐ I have gotten in trouble for the way I behave or speak to others.

☐ Others say I always want things my way and don't compromise.

Total: _____

Passive-Aggressive

☐ I tend to be sarcastic a lot or complain about people behind their backs.

☐ When I am upset, I often ignore people or walk away, and even slam doors.

☐ After I agree to do something, I am often resentful and complain.

☐ I rarely express how I feel directly, because I fear upsetting others. Instead I convey hurt feelings indirectly; for example, by being late, forgetful, or letting someone down.

☐ I tend to hold grudges and save up hurt feelings to let them all out during later arguments.

Total: _____

Assertive

☐ I know I have the right to express my feelings and opinions, and I express them clearly and directly.

☐ I listen to what other people have to say and try to validate their feelings and perspectives.

☐ When we have different goals, I try to negotiate a reasonable compromise instead of just trying to win or get my way.

☐ I do not cave to the views or decisions of others, or insist that things need to be viewed my way.

☐ When people treat me unfairly, I explain how their behavior made me feel and how I would like to be treated.

Total: _____

skill practice: assertiveness

As you have seen, assertiveness can be a very important interpersonal skill. It is the balanced way of standing up for yourself without stepping on someone else. How exactly do you practice assertiveness? Follow these steps and try it out.

1. Explain the issue clearly.

    Assertiveness is about standing up for yourself, including what you want, what you believe in, and what you don't want. It can be asking someone for something, like a ride or permission to go out. Or it can be saying no to something, like letting your friend copy your homework. So the first question is, what is the issue? Before you have the discussion with the other person, decide what you want the outcome to be. Then explain clearly and honestly what you have to say.

2. Honestly express how you feel.

    This helps the other person understand the feelings behind the difficulty you are having. Describe how you feel instead of directing blame to the other person. Focus on positive feelings related to your goals if you can, not on your resentment of the other person.

3. Describe the change you want.

    Clearly explain the change you would like to see. Be specific about what action should stop (for example, your brother's teasing) or start (for example, a friend's cooperating). Be sure the requested changes are reasonable, consider the other person's needs, and be willing to make changes yourself in return.

4. Listen and validate.

Once you have described the issue, your feelings, and the changes you hope for, give the other person a chance to share. Listen to what the person has to say without reacting. Validate his or her feelings about the issue.

5. Negotiate.

Now that you have heard both sides, it's time to negotiate. Try to figure out what is reasonable for both of you. Be fair to yourself and the other person.

6. Act on values.

Remember your values and intentions. Do not compromise your values for someone else, because that will lower your own self-esteem.

exercise: assertiveness practice

Think of situations with others that have been difficult to handle lately. Focus on one where your communication was passive, aggressive, or passive-aggressive.

Describe the situation.

_____

_____

What did you do?

_____

_____

Would the way you handled the situation be considered passive, aggressive, or passive-aggressive?

_____

_____

For each numbered step described earlier, what could you have said or done in order to be more assertive?

1. <u>Explain the issue:</u> _____

_____

2. <u>Express how you feel:</u> _____

_____

3. <u>Describe the change:</u> _____

_____

4. <u>Listen and validate:</u> _____

_____

5. <u>Negotiate:</u> _____

_____

6. <u>Act on values:</u> _____

_____

If possible, practice the assertiveness steps you listed in a real-life situation.

What was the outcome?

_____

_____

_____

How did it feel to be assertive?

_____

_____

_____

45 using I-messages

When we are angry with someone else, we often show we are mad instead of explaining how we feel. We might slam doors, yell, or storm off and pout. When your out-of-control behaviors show how upset you are, you leave the other person with only two choices—to push back and control your behavior, or cave to your threats. Neither response leads to cooperation or mutual understanding.

Explaining how you feel to the person you are having a conflict with can be a bridge toward mutual understanding. Even if you just say them in your head, simply starting off with the words "I feel…" will calm you by naming your true feelings. These words will direct your attention to your inner experience, rather than outward against the other person. Saying how you really feel may make you feel vulnerable; it may feel safer to stay in attack mode. But if you want the other person to truly understand how you feel, you need to be able to explain openly without threat.

Using *I-messages* instead of you-messages is an important way to improve communication skills. You-messages focus on what other people have done in a way that makes them feel attacked. These messages usually include words like "You always (never, should, must)…" When people hear these kinds of accusations, they stop listening and become defensive.

Without blaming others, an I-message explains what you feel, what the other person may have done that led to your feeling that way, and why you feel the way you do. When you use an I-message, you take responsibility for your emotions, which is less likely to make the other person defensive. This approach reduces blame, making it easier to work out a solution.

exercise: changing you-messages to I-messages

For each situation, write down how you would respond using a you-message. Then change the statement to a more helpful I-message.

Example: Your mom promised to give you a ride to meet your friends at the movies, but she gets home late, and you are going to be fifteen minutes late to meet your friends.

You-message: You're always late. You don't care about me at all.

I-message: I feel mad when you are late because it makes me think you don't care about my social life, and I get anxious about missing my friends.

You try to talk to your friend when you are really upset, but the whole time she is texting and not paying much attention to you.

You-message: _____

I-message: _____

You really want to go to your friend's party, but your dad tells you no because the parents will not be there, and he is worried something will happen to you.

You-message: _____

I-message: _____

Your brother takes your iPod without your permission, and now he's afraid he lost it.

You-message: _____

I-message: _____

skill practice: using I-messages

During the next week, practice using I-messages. Start with easier situations, gradually moving toward situations where there is more conflict. Follow these steps:

- Turn your attention inward to be clear about what you are feeling. (Use RAIN to help.)

- Be clear about what is causing you to feel that way. What specific behaviors or actions caused you to react with these feelings?

- Deliver your I-message. Pick a time when things are calm.
  State clearly and directly: *I feel _____ when _____ because _____.*

- Congratulate yourself on expressing how you feel (regardless of the response you get).

responding to pain with compassion 46

Having compassion is about caring for our pain and the pain of others without needing it to go away or fixing it. People often find it easier to be compassionate toward others and what they are going through. Having compassion for ourselves can be tough, but the care of compassion needs to start in our own hearts.

Try to repeat these words for five minutes a day and throughout the day.

May I understand this anger.

May this anger and frustration lessen.

May I feel calm and at ease regardless of the situation.

formal practice: loving-kindness meditation

The written instructions below are a simplified version of the full guided meditation that can be downloaded at http://www.newharbinger.com/29163. We recommend that you listen to the audio recording to get the full benefits of this meditation. Get started with these basic steps. Pause for a few minutes between each step.

You can do this practice very easily. Read these phrases again and again, slowly thinking of each word. Notice what comes up in your heart and mind. If you practice this meditation, you will begin to retrain your brain to respond differently. It works. Give it a try. We dare you!

- *May I feel safe and free from inner and outer harm.*

May I let go of anger and be peaceful and at ease.

May I be free from suffering and the causes of suffering.

May I be happy and be connected to the root of happiness.

May I have courage and grace.

May I be free.

- *May we all feel safe and free from inner and outer harm.*

May we be peaceful and at ease.

May we be free from suffering and the causes of suffering.

May we be happy and be connected to the root of happiness.

May we have courage and grace.

May we be free.

- *May our "difficult ones" feel safe and free from inner and outer harm.*

May they be peaceful and at ease.

May they be free from suffering and the causes of suffering.

May they be happy and be connected to the root of happiness.

May they have courage and grace.

May they be free.

- *May all beings be free.*

putting it all together

Take a few minutes to complete this self-assessment. See if you have been able to make some changes in your life with some of the new skills you have learned. Check off the statements that are true of you.

understanding my anger patterns

Knowing which anger style you tend to rely on can be a big step toward self-understanding. It helps you feel like you are not alone; there are other people out there who handle their anger similarly. Identifying your anger patterns can also help you figure out which skills you may need to focus on.

☐ I understand some of the roots of my anger.

☐ I am aware of my fight-or-flight response and remind myself that I am safe.

☐ I understand my anger cycle.

☐ I avoid power struggles.

mindfulness

Like many other skills in life—exercise, art, or learning, for example—what you get out of mindfulness will depend on how much you put in. With practice, you will develop a better ability to be "with" your experience, even when you encounter conflict.

☐ I understand what mindfulness is.

☐ I can name three informal mindfulness skills I use.

☐ I understand the meaning of having a wise mind.

☐ I regularly do a formal mindfulness meditation practice.

changing anger patterns

Change starts with commitment. In reading this book, you already made that commitment. And by better understanding your anger, you can make better choices.

☐ I can track my anger patterns; for example, by using anger maps.

☐ I can identify my thoughts, feelings, and sensations when I get angry; for example, by keeping a CALM log.

☐ I respond mindfully instead of acting on aggressive urges.

body-calming strategies

The physical body can be an important instrument for managing your anger. Learning to observe the early signs can slow angry reactions. Developing skills for tolerating and redirecting this physical energy can prevent many angry outbursts.

☐ I know my anger alarm and the signs of anger in my body.

☐ I can slow down anger rising in my body.

☐ I have five strategies to calm myself when my anger is overwhelming.

mental clarity skills

How you think can play a major part in how you see the world and what you choose to do. Mental clarity can free you from operating on angry autopilot and allow you to choose how to view the world around you.

- [ ] I know my own mental traps that get me more angry.

- [ ] I am now able to think more clearly when I start to get upset.

emotional balance

Emotions can feel powerful and overwhelming and often lead to a vicious cycle. Upsetting feelings lead to out-of-control behaviors that cause more upsetting feelings, and on and on. With practice, you can achieve better emotional balance.

- [ ] I take better care of my emotional health.

- [ ] I am aware of emotional triggers that upset me.

- [ ] I am better able to identify the true feelings beneath my anger.

making connections

Patterns of relating to others may be hard to change, but it can be done. Although kindness and understanding are not always easy, they can be the start of a happier way of living.

- [ ] I try to see both sides of a conflict, using *and* instead of *but*.

- [ ] I am more assertive and use I-messages more often than you-messages.

- [ ] I am more compassionate and understanding toward myself and others.

Take a look at what you checked off. Congratulate yourself on the changes you have made. This book has a whole lot of skills and ideas in it. We don't expect anyone to remember them all or be able to use them all the time. If there were boxes you couldn't check off, that's okay. Ask yourself, *Was I unable to check that one because I don't know it, or because I don't practice it?* Go back to that section of the book and see if it makes sense the second time. See if you can make an effort to practice it now.

We're sure you now understand that anger won't just magically disappear; it takes effort and awareness to manage. Our hope is that you have gained some skills and awareness that you can continue to practice as anger invitations come up in your life. We wholeheartedly wish you the best for a life with less anger and more happiness. After all, this is the only life you have. Why not enjoy it?

reference list

Linehan, M. 1993. *Cognitive-Behavioral Treatment of Borderline Personality Disorder.* New York: Guilford Press.

Nelson, P. 1993. *There's a Hole in My Sidewalk: The Romance of Self-Discovery.* New York: Atria Publishing Group (Beyond Words Publishing).

Potter-Efron, R., and P. Potter-Efron. 2006. *Letting Go of Anger.* Oakland, CA: New Harbinger Publications.

Stahl, B., and E. Goldstein. 2010. *A Mindfulness-Based Stress Reduction Workbook.* Oakland, CA: New Harbinger Publications.

Mark Purcell, MEd, PsyD, is a licensed clinical psychologist who has worked with youth and families for the past twenty years. Purcell has developed DBT programs for youth agencies and trains mental health professionals in a variety of settings. He is a professor in the department of psychology at John F. Kennedy University and has a private practice in the San Francisco Peninsula.

Jason R. Murphy, MA, is a mindfulness based psychotherapist and meditation teacher who has worked with youth and families for the past twenty years. Murphy has been practicing *Vipassana* (Insight) meditation since 1994 and is a teacher in that tradition. He is a certified addictions counselor and founder of Mindfulness Recovery Counseling. Murphy has taught mindful awareness in a variety of settings around the United States. Murphy's particular focus has been working with youth and incarcerated men and women addressing issues of stress, anger, and addiction. He is in private practice and leads groups and workshops in Santa Cruz, CA.

Register your **new harbinger** titles for additional benefits!

When you register your **new harbinger** title—purchased in any format, from any source—you get access to benefits like the following:

- Downloadable accessories like printable worksheets and extra content

- Instructional videos and audio files

- Information about updates, corrections, and new editions

Not every title has accessories, but we're adding new material all the time.

Access free accessories in 3 easy steps:

1. Sign in at NewHarbinger.com (or **register** to create an account).

2. Click on **register a book**. Search for your title and click the **register** button when it appears.

3. Click on the **book cover or title** to go to its details page. Click on **accessories** to view and access files.

That's all there is to it!

If you need help, visit:

NewHarbinger.com/accessories

new harbinger
CELEBRATING
40 YEARS

FROM OUR PUBLISHER—

As the publisher at New Harbinger and a clinical psychologist since 1978, I know that emotional problems are best helped with evidence-based therapies. These are the treatments derived from scientific research (randomized controlled trials) that show what works. Whether these treatments are delivered by trained clinicians or found in a self-help book, they are designed to provide you with proven strategies to overcome your problem.

Therapies that aren't evidence-based—whether offered by clinicians or in books—are much less likely to help. In fact, therapies that aren't guided by science may not help you at all. That's why this New Harbinger book is based on scientific evidence that the treatment can relieve emotional pain.

This is important: if this book isn't enough, and you need the help of a skilled therapist, use the following resource to find a clinician trained in the evidence-based protocols appropriate for your problem.

Real help is available for the problems you have been struggling with. The skills you can learn from evidence-based therapies will change your life.

Matthew McKay, PhD
Publisher, New Harbinger Publications

If you need a therapist, the following organization can help you find a therapist trained in cognitive behavioral therapy (CBT).

The Association for Behavioral & Cognitive Therapies (ABCT) Find-a-Therapist service offers a list of therapists schooled in CBT techniques. Therapists listed are licensed professionals who have met the membership requirements of ABCT and who have chosen to appear in the directory.

Please visit www.abct.org and click on *Find a Therapist*.

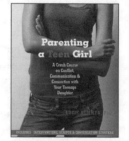